LOVE, LUST AND LOGIC

A GUIDE TO REAL RELATIONSHIPS

LEAH KAY ROSSI

FAMILY & RELATIONSHIPS / Dating

FAMILY & RELATIONSHIPS / Love & Romance

Special discounts are available on quantity purchases by corporations, associations and others. For details, contact the author.

The information in this book is not intended to replace the advice of a physician. It is for informational purposes only and any mental health suggestion should be started under the advisement of a licensed physician or professional.

Neither the author nor the publisher assumes any responsibility or liability whatsoever on behalf of the consumer or reader of this material. Any perceived slight of any individual or organization is purely unintentional.

DO YOU HAVE A MESSAGE TO SHARE WITH THE WORLD?
ARE YOU INTERESTED IN HAVING YOUR BOOK PUBLISHED?
VISIT ZAMIZPRESS.COM

All rights reserved. No part of this publication may be reproduced, distributed or transmitted in any form or by any means, including photocopying, recording, or other electronic or mechanical methods, without the prior written permission of the publisher, except in the case of brief quotations embodied in critical reviews and certain other noncommercial uses permitted by copyright law.

Copyright © 2022 by Leah Kay Rossi

Cover design by Nathaniel Dasco

All rights reserved.

Love, Lust and Logic: A Guide to Real Relationships / Leah Kay Rossi — 1st Edition

ISBN: 978-1-949813-16-6

ISBN: 978-1-949813-17-3

CONTENTS

1. Are You Ready? — 1
2. Let's Call it Love — 5
3. When Surface Level Won't Do — 9
4. Get Ready — 11
   Let's Love List
5. Relationship Role Models — 21
   the Bundys or the Bradys
6. Attachment and Connection — 25
   Velcro or Hang on Loosely?
7. Attention, Respect, & Expectations — 29
   Give it to Get it
8. Finances — 35
   This Can Tank Your Relationship
9. Fidelity & Honesty — 47
   Sinner or Saint?
10. Mental Health — 53
    Let's Talk About It
11. Alcohol and Drug Use — 61
    Bottoms Up or Down?
12. Manners, Politeness, & Patience — 67
    Ask Dear Abby
13. Fighting Style — 73
    MMA or WWF?
14. Do You Pretzel? — 77
    It's Time to Untwist
15. Friends — 81
    I'll Be There for You
16. Religion and Politics — 87
    A No-No at Parties
17. Sex — 91
    Basic Instinct
18. Lawless — 103
    Brushes with the Law
19. Live Together — 107
    Go All In or Wait Till Marriage?
20. Marriage, In-laws, & Family — 111
    Till Death Do Us Part

21. **Children** *Blessed Event*	123
22. **Household Dynamics** *Who Was in Your House?*	127
23. **Pets** *Fur or No Fur?*	137
24. **Real Life Situations** *When S*&% Hits the Fan*	141
25. **Dissection of A Red Flag** *(ARF)*	147
26. **Deal Breakers**	163
27. **Wrap it Up**	165
References	167
Acknowledgments	169
About the Author	171

1
ARE YOU READY?

Get ready to read, self-evaluate and write! Asking questions, evaluating answers and observing others is how I believe we learn to make educated decisions about people, partners and relationships.

The most important questions start within us. Are you ready for love and commitment? If so, opening your heart means being vulnerable, but also being wise.

Are you ready to take the time to truly learn about yourself as well as your partner? Has your pattern been bonding thru sex or falling in love too quickly? As women we have a much greater tendency to bond after just one sexual encounter with a partner. We may even start envisioning a life together. Be honest, you know you've done it.

Technology has created some social norms that we need to avoid. There are many unanswered questions when we move too fast. Slow down. We don't have to rush through potential partners thinking we are missing out, if you and I don't go fast enough. Do you rush to swipe right, swipe left, or maybe you don't swipe at all? Spending time with someone and truly getting to know them helps you to evaluate if that person is truly compatible with you. Look into their eyes, do their eyes meet yours?

We are going to do our "self" homework. I know what you're thinking, I have! Let's make sure by reading and answering the questions inside and if you have a partner, ask them the questions as well. You can learn at a deep level about yourself, your partner and the potential of a lasting relationship in these pages.

All couples have differing opinions on certain topics, but typically you and your partner's beliefs will need to be similar for more relationship success. Deep commitments come with the intimacy of full disclosure, along with shared values and ideals.

If we initially fall in love, infatuation or lust due to chemistry, limbic bonding (sex), loneliness or neediness, those infatuation or lust feelings can fade quickly. A relationship that starts this way may not be grounded in truly knowing each other, real acceptance and trust.

Let's analyze what you want and need from a partner and a relationship by putting together your love list and deal breakers. This is real life, not the unrealistic romantic movies the media has fed us. No, *Cinderella* and *Pretty Woman* are not real. It is magical when you know someone loves you unconditionally with emotional warts and all.

Being in love was like a drug for me. It was the only time I felt "good enough" but that feeling was always fleeting. I didn't realize the impact of not having a father or having good relationship role models until I had suffered through several dysfunctional relationships.

Most of the population has had at least one of the issues or experiences listed below. These make navigating dating, relationships and choosing a suitable partner extra challenging.

1. Absentee parent or abandonment
2. Poor relationship role models
3. Living in fear of abuse, poverty, etc.
4. Divorce of parents
5. Childhood trauma

6. Low self-esteem or mental health issues
7. Addiction (family member or themselves)

If any of the issues listed are left without the proper care, a repeated pattern of behavior and choices could continue.

I experienced five of the seven issues listed. Boundaries were non-existent in my past relationships and I kept the "denial goggles" on when faced with red flags. These red flags should have been deal breakers. This unfortunate pattern continued until I got right with myself. Learning that my thoughts were powerful and that what I chose to believe in became my reality was such an epiphany. Choosing to believe I was worthy instead of worthless began a transformation in me. Letting go of my past is a daily, ongoing, process.

You need to be good with yourself when you are looking for love. Generally, we tend to attract what we think about and believe will happen. If you are optimistic you will most likely attract someone who is also optimistic. Wrap your head around that one...all the way. We have to be willing to do some self-discovery and take accountability for what might need improving whether we created the issue or it was thrust upon us.

Relationship counselor Marisa Peer says it perfectly, "You need to put your effort into falling in love with you and then the world will change so dramatically."

Let me ask: Are you "right" with yourself? Do you love yourself? We need to be sure, because it is difficult to give love or receive love when we don't love ourselves.

Get a pen, or if you want to erase, grab a pencil and get ready to write. Write your own answers and if you have a partner courageously ask them the questions and log the answers in this book. Putting down your own answers, along with your partner's, gives you an opportunity to reflect on the answers.

Answer honestly, or there will be no point in answering at all. There are no right or wrong answers. The questions are here to help you learn about yourself and what your partner's views and life experiences are. This can create an open line of communication, create trust and allow safe vulnerability. You can also ask deeper, thought-provoking questions to create more intimacy.

Feel free to skip around to different chapters when you are asking your partner some of the questions, depending on the length and depth of your relationship.

Are you ready? Here we go!

2

LET'S CALL IT LOVE

So, you think you are in love? Yeah, me too, too many times to count, but what stuck for me? Nothing stuck because there wasn't a real foundation to stick to. It took a long time for me to figure out that "I" was half of the problem. Funny, how easy it is to blame your partner for the demise of a relationship. It usually takes two. However, certain situations can vary the percentages vastly. For example: if one of the partners has been unfaithful. The mixtures of reasons and percentages could go on forever. The bottom line is, until you are "right" with you, you'll have difficulty selecting a suitable partner and having an effective, healthy relationship.

If we fall too fast in lust or bonded love by the time we get to the real Q & A it may be too late. By then, it doesn't matter what the answers are because we only hear what we want to...hence the avoidance of a Red Flag. (We will refer to A Red Flag from this point forward as an ARF.)

You're in love...

True love, the real deal, is bliss, right?

The feeling is amazing, fantastical, and you never want the feeling to end.

You know that they are "the one."

They are your person. Your forever.
They complete you. (Hmmmm, sound familiar?)
How do you know this?
Is it because you're attracted to them?
Is it chemistry?
Do you like the same things?
Do you share common values?

Yes, these are the general ways we determine if we like someone and want to be around them. During the beginning of a relationship, we learn about the other person by asking questions, getting answers and observing their behaviors and actions.

During the beginning Q & A, we share our common answers easily and with glee. We tend to avoid the ones that might not fit, for fear of rejection. It is so simple and easy, right?

HIM: "Do you like to go camping?"
HER: "Yes, I love camping."
HIM: "Me too."

Check. Like checking off a box on a list.

Unfortunately, most of these questions are surface level. They are the basic fluff that sticks and pulls you closer to that person.

Let's be honest, we all want to be liked and accepted, so do we always answer with complete accuracy?

HER: "Yeah, sure I like camping." If camping means a hotel with room service, then yes, she loves camping.

Or "Sure, I loved growing up in a big family." When in actuality, you hated it because you felt anonymous.

Or better yet, he asks, "I go to the gym 3-5 times a week. Do you like to work out?"

"Oh my gosh! Me too, I love the gym!" She replies.

If by the gym, you mean the spa, then I like going to the spa 3-5 times a week for a facial, manicure or pedicure. They have a masseuse at the gym, right?

If you lie or get lied to with common interests, then what might be next? Values, past relationships, faithfulness, mental health. Where does it end?

Look at any dating site and you will find this common topic. It's my favorite example:

"Do you like to go hiking?" He asks.

"Yes, I try to go hiking every weekend," she replies.

He's beyond elated that he's found someone who shares his passion for hiking, but actually this equals:

HER: I'll go hiking until he falls in love with me. If he loves me, he won't mind if I don't want to go hiking anymore.

HIM: I feel defrauded by you. You attracted me by deceitfully telling me you had a common interest.

Resentment can build at some point, even if he does fall in love with you. The truth is you don't have to like everything they do. It's unrealistic to think you will or should.

Be honest, if you hate hiking fine. Hiking is something that he can do with his friends. You could compromise and go hiking every couple of months. If hiking is a deal breaker, then so be it.

We are constantly changing and growing in what we might want or need in a partner as time passes. When you're in your 20's and 30's chemistry and ambition may have been your priority.

In your 50's and 60's you might be looking for someone with common hobbies and overall companionship.

Deal Breakers

Stop and think about it. Do you have a list of deal breakers? You should. If you don't, you may compromise something you could seriously regret later or become a pretzel. A pretzel is trying to be everything you "think" the other person wants or needs.

There will always be challenges in life with or without a partner. You need to decide what you are not willing to accept in your partner or relationship. Those are your deal breakers. For me, a deal breaker would be someone who has an addictive habit.

Having deal breakers means you have boundaries. Boundaries are necessary for healthy relationships. Deal breakers could be anything from not wanting to be with someone who smokes cigarettes to having a different religion. Deal breakers are very personal and should not be superficial in nature, they should have conviction in what you truly need.

Obviously, common interests are important, as are similar values and life goals. However, there are plenty of areas where differences are needed and should be respected and valued. Differences can balance out a relationship.

It can be easy to say "I love you" when you have physical chemistry chemistry, and your limbic system (brain chemistry) is bonding. But without truly getting to know your partner, an "I love you" isn't enough to really cement a relationship. Some people say "I love you" after the first hello, first kiss, the first date, or the first sexual encounter. Some people easily fall in love, while others avoid it at all costs. Falling too fast is risky and can end up in heartache.

Saying the words "I love you" doesn't have real meaning without truly knowing your partners flaws and accepting them "as is," as you would want to be accepted. True, real love and intimacy is created by being vulnerable.

It's crucial to be open to touchy topics of discussion, like fidelity, finances, and expectations. It is important to truly understanding your potential partner or current relationship.

Expectations can be relationship bonfire. If you or your partner have unrealistic, fantasy-like expectations, you may never genuinely be in love or fulfilled in your relationship.

What was your biggest takeaway from this chapter?

3

WHEN SURFACE LEVEL WON'T DO

Most people don't initially ask the challenging questions. They usually come about due to an event or circumstance that presents itself. Once you're in a mutually exclusive relationship, digging below the surface and asking challenging questions can offer insight into how this person you adore became who they are. When you're young, your life experiences are usually impacted by your family, beginning with your parents. The person who raised you, whether it was your parents, grandparents, etc., are your examples and reflection.

The experiences you have growing up reflect a set of ideals and beliefs. The memories of your upbringing generally shape the sort of values you want in your partner as well as the type of parent you want to be.

If there is a deep reoccurring cycle, it might repeat itself for generations. Or you can choose to break that cycle. Cycles like neglect, emotional, or physical abuse can and should be broken.

My household was just me and my mom. My mom was raised in a strict German household. Her mother never spoke to her about relationships and she never spoke to me about men, dating, sex, relationships, love, or money. My mom's first marriage ended before I was two and her second marriage, when I was thirteen, lasted one year. My mother was amazing, worked hard and provided a lower-middle-class life for us. Doing this took all her energy, day in and day out. She spent the rest of her life without a partner. For me this meant I had a lack of knowledge and I was riddled with the fear of being alone like my mom.

As a teen and young adult, I learned a lot "on the street" from friends and boys. Because I lacked self-esteem, it made me an easy target to be taken advantage of. Many years later the pieces fell together and I understood how my upbringing had drastically impacted my life.

It's a funky blend of inherited genes, personality traits, life experiences and modeled behavior that then creates our unique selves. Nothing creates us more than our own thoughts, beliefs, and perceptions. It is overwhelmingly powerful to change your thoughts and beliefs. Even more powerful can be the moment when you realize this and utilize that power for a positive outcome. Each of us has the power to do it; it just depends on whether or not you choose to use it. What you think about, you truly bring about.

What was your biggest takeaway from this chapter?

4

GET READY
LET'S LOVE LIST

Trust is the main foundation in a committed relationship. If you allow yourself to trust and be worthy of trust, a bond can form that strengthens intimacy and deepens closeness. Being accepted for who you are builds trust and unconditional love. Knowing and loving someone to an unconditional depth takes emotional maturity and, more importantly, vulnerability. The greatest forms of love come from complete vulnerability and unwavering trust. As Dr. Sue Johnson so precisely put it,

"We are never so vulnerable as when we love."

When someone asks you a question, you think, retrieve, perceive, and sometimes contrast what you want against what you have, before you come to your final answer. This usually depends on the depth of the question. It's an easy, quick answer if someone asks you if you like ice cream. It's altogether different if someone asks you why you don't have a relationship with your mother.

Consider the following questions and write down your answers:

Can you share deep parts of who you are with others without the fear of judgment or loss?

Do you have the courage to be vulnerable?

Do you lie or withhold information, hoping the truth never comes out?

These are soul-searching questions that will ultimately determine if you are willing to dig deeper and gain the benefits of doing so.

Here's a sample dialogue that could open up other thought-provoking topics:

You: "What is one of your childhood memories that seemed different or strange and why?"

Partner: "There was a time when I was around thirteen that my mom stopped going to the grocery store. She would send me to the market, with a list and cash. Since I was underage, I could not buy her cigarettes or wine. I really don't know why she couldn't go to the market anymore; I figured she was just tired from working all day and being a single mom."

You: "I'm sorry you had to go alone since you didn't have any siblings. That seems like a lot to put on a young teenager. Were you scared?"

. . .

Partner: "Thank you for caring. I didn't realize it was a lot for my age. I don't remember being scared, perhaps because I was just used to being alone and handling things."

You: "You mentioned you could not buy wine and cigarettes. Do you think your mom smoke or drank too much? My dad did. He was a chain-smoker who drank way too much beer."

Hopefully, this dialogue example can give you some ideas to develop a conversation of your own.

The following questions can lead to additional topics while learning about each other's past and upbringing:

What is your most treasured memory?

What is your worst memory?

What were the three things you were most grateful for as a child?
  1.)
  2.)
  3.)

What are the three things that you are most grateful for now?
  1.)
  2.)
  3.)

. . .

What are the top three values you have that are most important to you? (Ex: honesty, work ethic, optimism, etc.)

1.)
2.)
3.)

The Love Lists: "Needs to Be" "Nice to Have" and "Icing"

Creating love lists focuses on which traits and qualities your partner has that are truly important to you. The most significant traits and qualities would be on your "needs to have" list. "Needs to have" are similar to deal breakers. Creating love lists isn't to rule out someone who might not have all the qualities you find important. No one is perfect and if you keep waiting for that perfect person, you will most likely end up very lonely. It's sort of like waiting to have children until you have enough money saved. If everyone waited, the population growth will slow to a crawl.

For example, a few "needs to be" for me are:

1. Honesty
2. An addiction free, healthy, lifestyle
3. The same belief system

Below are some ideas that might help you create your "needs to be" love list. Circle and write down your top five "needs to be" qualities below the traits mentioned:

Honest
Dependable
Calm
Faithful
Workaholic

Responsible
Ethical
Passionate
Patient
Kind
Secure
Family-oriented
Confident
Compassionate
Leader
Selfless
Optimistic
Artistic
Grateful
Earthy
Risk-taker
Ambitious
Romantic
Practical
Humble
Dreamer
Inventor
Traditional
Unconventional
Free-Spirit
Generous
Thoughtful
Good sense of humor
Good
Morals
Spiritual
Introspective
Forgiving
Organized
Active

Adventurous
Grounded
Extrovert
Easy-going
Introvert
Healthy lifestyle
Empathetic
Non-judgmental
Understanding
Belief/faith
Balanced
Fair
Competitive
Helpful
Energetic
1.
2.
3.
4.
5.

The next love list is the "nice to have" list which encompasses facets you would deeply appreciate in your partner. These aren't mandatory, but would enhance your compatibility.

Below are some ideas that might help in creating your "nice to have" love list. For example, a "nice to have" would be several shared interests or hobbies.

Write your top five "nice to haves" below these ideas:
Volunteer/Service
Theater/Plays
Symphony
Live Music/Concerts

Dancing
Stand-up comedy
Books/Reading
Camping
Off-roading
Cooking
Shopping
Antiquing
Snow skiing
Bicycling
Wine-tasting
Motorcycles
Hiking
Running/Jogging
Water sports/Skiing
Boating
Fishing
Hunting/Shooting
Decorating
Tennis
Board games
Movies
TV watching
Dining out
Travel
Traveling abroad
Cruise ships
Nightclubs
Singing/Karaoke
Gym/Working out
Yoga
Crafting
DIY/Home improvement
Beach
Surfing

Golfing
Bowling
Sporting events
Gaming
Ballet
Entertaining
Restoration
Car buff
Card games/Poker
Meditation
Photography
Scuba diving/Snorkeling
Morning person
Night owl
Sarcastic sense of humor
Large extended family
Punctual
Enjoy same music genres
Dry sense of humor
Financial smarts
Goofy sense of humor
Technology savvy
Survival skills
Mechanically inclined

For me, a few "nice to haves" would be:

1. Likes to dance
2. Has a goofy sense of humor
3. Enjoys live music and concerts

1.
2.
3.

4.
5.

The last love list is called "icing," which are bonus items your partner might have that are like icing on a great cake. Again, these are not items to weed out potential partners, but to see what you might consider a bonus.

Here are some ideas to help create your "icing" love list. Write your top three "icing" items after these ideas:
Speaks more than one language
Self-employed
Fan of the same sports team
Vegan
Musically inclined
West Coast swing dancer

For me "icing" would be:

1. Speaks Spanish
2. Self-employed
3. Loves to cook (I am not a fan of cooking.)

1.
2.
3.

Keep this book handy so you can easily add, delete, or change it if something comes to mind.

. . .

What was your biggest takeaway from this chapter?

The following chapters are categories of relationship questions as well as traits and behaviors to observe. These questions encourage you to learn about yourself in specific relationship situations and will help you put together your "deal breaker" list as well as open your eyes to any potential ARFs (A Red Flag) before you are in too deep.

5
RELATIONSHIP ROLE MODELS
THE BUNDYS OR THE BRADYS

Generally, we model those around us growing up. Usually, it's our parent(s), grandparents or other relatives whom we observe, that our relationships are patterned after. However, if those observations left you feeling bad, you might want to break those patterns in your own relationships. Or, you could have wonderful relationship role models that you hope to duplicate in your own life.

Contrast can also happen after spending time outside our own families. This contrast can be huge or slight, depending on the area of the relationship. Relationship role models aren't perfect. Hopefully, after examining your own models, you can take the best practices from what you've witnessed and add in what you felt was missing.

Respect, affection, disagreement resolution, and parenting styles are the main parts of relationship role models. I didn't have a normal household to imitate; therefore, my expectations were very skewed. Be honest with yourself as you search your past. Sometimes we choose to gloss over parts of our childhood or block out what we want to forget. However, those memories can be learned from, especially if you want to break a negative cycle. If necessary, consult a qualified, highly-skilled therapist to work on your past and see if you are unwittingly repeating a negative pattern.

Questions:

Whom did you model, parents, grandparents, parents of friends, extended family members, television, movies, books?

Whom would you like to model now? Is it someone different than before?

What are the positive aspects you want to duplicate?

Were your role models respectful?

Faithful?

Honest?

Loving and affectionate?

Considerate?

What are some negatives traits you want to avoid?

Being overly critical or demeaning?

Name calling or a spiteful tone?

Unsupportive?

Unaffectionate?

What did you think was missing from the role models you were exposed to?

Why?

Are there cycles you want to break?

If you could change an aspect of how you were raised, what would it be?

My friend's parents were married for over twenty years before getting divorced and were completely miserable. They stayed together for the children. The kids hated them together and especially hated listening to the constant, toxic, fighting.

How did your relationship role models deal with disagreements?

Did they use you or your siblings as pawns during arguments?

. . .

Did they blame you or your siblings (as children) for their fighting?

Did arguing or fighting seem normal?

My relationship contrast came from the television show *The Brady Bunch*. Google it and watch an episode if you haven't seen it. It is an iconic 70's television show. A widow and widower meet, marry, and blend their six kids perfectly, like the miracle it was. The mom stays home and has a housekeeper. The dad works and supports the family of nine as an architect.

Obviously, *The Brady Bunch* is unrealistic in some fashion, but it also showed ways to deal with mishaps in a loving and fair manner. The children are taught to respect their parents, teachers, and elders. Parents never yelled. It illustrated the large family dynamic I lacked. Plus, like everyone else, I wanted to be Marsha, the hip, cool chick.

What was your biggest takeaway from this chapter?

6
ATTACHMENT AND CONNECTION
VELCRO OR HANG ON LOOSELY?

Attachment and connection levels vary depending on the needs each person has. Think about what you need from a partner in reference to the following:

How much reassurance do you need?

> None
> Daily
> Weekly
> On occasion
> After an argument

How often do you need affirmations of love?

> Daily
> Weekly
> On occasion

Dr. Gary Chapman's book *The Five Love Languages* goes into great depth about the ways we feel loved, whether it is through words of affirmation, physical touch, gift-giving, actions, or quality time. Most people have two of the five love languages that speak to them predominantly.

What makes you feel most loved?

Words of affirmation like I love you, compliments, and appreciation?

Showing you love by taking action--by planning and doing things for you like washing your car or doing the laundry?

Is it touch like, holding your hand, putting an arm around you, physical closeness and affection?

Do you enjoy gift giving? Do you want them to buy you flowers, a coffee, or the simple things you know would make life easier?

Is your language spending quality time together, uninterrupted, one-on-one, focused time?

Learning how someone feels connected and loved is like unlocking the mysterious relationship genie. The relationship genie decodes what your partner needs in order to feel loved and gives you the knowledge to provide it.

. . .

Some people may need words of reassurance and physical touch to feel loved. Others might need to be shown love with acts of service, like doing the dishes or making the bed each day.

Knowing what your partner needs is the just the beginning. Taking action toward what your partner needs to feel loved takes maturity, selflessness, and commitment.

What's Your Communication Style?

How little or much communication do you need from your partner?

As needed?
Constant?
Texts or calls throughout the day?

Are you secure in yourself and your relationship without constant communication?

Are you insecure, needy or clingy?

Are you an anxious type?

If you are newly dating and your new person is clingy, needy or insecure, you might want to slow things down and find out why this person is behaving this way. Falling too hard and too fast can be a sign of low self-esteem and if you are the "rescuer type" you may find yourself attached before you even know it.

If both parties have low self-esteem, they might be drawn together and feed off each other's insecurities. They may also offer the quick "I love you," but then their relationship may end up filled with jealously and drama.

Hearing "I love you" right way can be scary and would make me run for the hills. This could be a borderline ARF. It takes time to truly love someone, especially unconditionally, quirks and all. True love comes with knowing someone intimately and deeply.

What was your biggest takeaway from this chapter?

7
ATTENTION, RESPECT, & EXPECTATIONS
GIVE IT TO GET IT

Attention

An attention request from your partner could be as simple as asking a question or making a comment. If they feel heard, and you feel heard, your connection deepens, and you're both likely to feel validated. If you share a meaningful story and your partner yawns or checks their phone, your bid for their attention has failed. This may be an indicator that your attention styles are not compatible or that your partner is self-involved.

Test this theory out on a first date. Did your date monitor their phone (excluding a babysitter or welfare check) on your date? Did they look at themselves in mirrors, or talk only about themselves? Those first couple of dates can really reveal a lot about someone's attention, listening, and awareness style.

Respect

Let me be very clear, a healthy relationship cannot exist without mutual respect.

It appears that many men want or need respect more than sex.

Feeling respected transcends all levels of emotion, including acceptance, power, and appreciation.

How about you, do you treat your partner's feelings, thoughts, and concerns with respect?

This doesn't mean you must always agree with your partner's thoughts or ideas, but that you honor their feelings and acknowledge them.

Watch how your partner treats their parents, siblings, boss, employees, co-workers, friends, strangers, elderly persons, service people, the law, and those less fortunate.

How someone treats others is a pretty accurate indicator of their character.

How do they treat other people?

Does your partner's boss get respect, but the waiter gets none?

Should the waiter be treated any differently than the boss?

Think about your own actions, do you treat people differently, if so whom and why?

Think about a boss you loved and a boss you hated. You probably treated the one you hated with as little respect as you could muster without getting fired, or maybe you did get fired. Then, think of the good boss you loved. Chances are high that they treated you with respect and genuine consideration, which you reflected in return.

Respectful communication during heated discussions should not consist of foul language, low blows, or name calling. Obviously, this can be extremely difficult if you are in anger overdrive. If you say hurtful things in the heat of the moment, you can't take them back. Period. End of story. Words can cut to the core. It's like trying to forget witnessing a horrible accident. You saw it and you can't unsee it.

Be respectful while asserting your concerns, hurts, or requests. It's easier to apologize for bad behavior after the fact. It's much, much harder to take control of your emotions and actions during the heat of an argument. However, you should take control and respectfully walk away, if necessary, and return later for a solution. It may not be easy to table an argument, but it could save you and your partner hurt and heartache if you do. In any relationship, if one or both parties feel disrespected, a pattern of disrespectful behavior may continue, and deep resentment could settle in.

I appreciate having my thoughts and feelings acknowledged by just active listening. I may be venting about a situation at work or the fact that my friend just found out she has breast cancer. You don't have to try and fix me or the issue. Just listen and be emotionally supportive.

To get respect you must give it.

Respect comes from being unselfish and unafraid to treat others the way you want to be treated. This generally produces respectful behavior in return. If it doesn't, you still know you are doing the right thing by living by The Golden Rule. Do unto others as you would want them to do unto you.

Expectations

The Golden Rule is easier to apply when there are clear expectations in your relationship. However, sometimes you or your partner can have the ever-elusive unknown expectations. This is where your partner just assumes you know what they want without clear communication. Making expectation assumptions can lead to a lot of misunderstanding and hurt.

You have to know the expectation before you can try to meet it.

How do you express your expectations?

When you don't know the other person's expectation, you have no way of meeting it, unless you are:
   a.) lucky as a leprechaun
   b.) a mind reader
   c.) so completely in sync with your lover that you always meet all their expectations.

Example

He asks, "What do you want for your birthday?"

She says, "Oh, nothing really. I don't really need anything, just save your money."

This really means:

"Buy me something I really want, and you would already know what that is, if you had been listening to me."

How do you handle and then express your disappointment if your expectation hasn't been met?

- Do you speak up?

How do you share your negative feelings or emotions?

- Do you bury your true feelings at all costs? (I'm pretty sure that causes cancer, doesn't everything?)
- Do you overreact?
- Do you berate the person for not knowing what you want or need?
- Do you sulk?
- Do you withhold affection?
- Can you share your concerns openly with sincere honesty?
- Can you make your expectations clearer for future understanding?

Talking about what you want, in a way your partner can actually hear you, is key. This isn't accomplished by complaining or shaming them into guilt. Ask with a respectful tone and kind words, the way you would want to be asked.

Just like teaching or parenting, if the child doesn't know what the expectations are, how are they supposed to meet them? Don't set your partner up to fail. Be mature and open and talk to your partner using positives and explain what your needs are and why.

Once reasonable expectations are clear, they should be easy to meet. Don't we all want to please the person we love the most?

What was your biggest takeaway from this chapter?

8

FINANCES

THIS CAN TANK YOUR RELATIONSHIP

Money, money, money, *MO-NEY, MO-NEY.* (Sing it like the hit song by the O'Jays.) Financial expectations, or any shared financial arrangement, should be addressed prior to marriage. Why? Because money issues are the number one reason for divorce.

Finances rule the divorce courts.

> The #1 **Reason** for **Divorce**? For decades, the **divorce** rate in America has hovered around fifty percent. ... In fact, some studies suggest that money problems in a marriage are the number **one cause of divorce**. The financial and emotional toll of a **divorce** can debilitate individuals and devastate families.[1]

I am still a huge believer in the "our" money philosophy—with a little twist. It doesn't matter who brings home the money, one or both, but it does matter how it is spent and on what. Those two decisions, how and what, are *critical*.

So, here's my twist on "our" money. As a couple, you have the bulk of your money in shared accounts. Then each person also has a separate account. This account contains a small portion of the money divided equally.

For example:
    Her monthly income is $4,000.00
    His monthly income is $4,000.00
    Total $8,000.00
    Their joint checking and savings accounts get $6,800.00
    The savings and household budget needs come first.
    Then the remaining $1,200.00 is split equally with $600.00 going to each separate account for individually directed expenditures.

Funds disbursement example:

- Savings account:
- Pay yourselves first: (percentage into savings account) savings for retirement, general savings, savings for a large purchase like a house, etc.
- Checking account:
- Pay household expenses: rent/mortgage, taxes, utilities, car loan, insurance, gas, food, etc.
- Savings or checking:
- Done together funds: entertainment, gifts for family, friends, vacation funds, etc.
- Individual separate account:
- Split leftover amount for individual personal spending.

For example: Her separate funds would pay for new leather boots or a manicure. His funds would pay for round of golf or a new fishing pole. These items are personal to them. So, if she wants to spend $200.00 on a pair of boots, it comes from her fund and not the grocery money. It allows for personal spending without resentment and judgement. This also applies to the non-income producing partner or spouse. If one person brings home all the money, the other still gets an equal allowance of the same amount.

Do you have a budget?

Do you stick to your budget?

Are you a saver?

Why?

Are you a spender?

Why?

Are you balanced?

Do you have a pattern with money?

How did you grow up, with money – upper class?

Middle class?

Lower middle class?

Without much money?

Was your family on government assistance?

Did you know about the state of your household finances growing up?

Did your parents appear to have money when they were actually in serious debt?

Did you hear your parents talk about money or money shortages?

Did you parents ever tell you "we can't afford that"?

Did your parents spoil you and buy you anything and everything?

Did you parents try to "keep up with the Joneses?"

Who was your money role model?

What is the purpose of money to you? Survival?

Security (retirement)?

. . .

Experiences (travel/good meals)?

Material items (big house, luxury car)?

What are your money priorities?

Do you save a percentage of your income every month?

Do you contribute to a retirement plan?

Are you willing to go without to save for a greater goal?

Are you spendthrift or frivolous?

Are you an impulse shopper?

Do you shop out of boredom or to fill a void?

Do you need to have the newest technology items, like the most recent iPhone, or gadget?

Do you donate money to charity?

. . .

Do you donate to church or tithe?

What are your debts?

Student loans? A car loan?

Credit cards?

If your debt is credit cards, what did you buy and why did you buy it?

What is your credit score?

Why is it high or low?

Have you filed bankruptcy?

If yes, why?

Do you know your partner's financial situation?

If you are established financially, should you ask for a prenuptial agreement?

. . .

A firm agreed-upon budget should be mandatory, and both parties need to adhere to it. If one person doesn't, it can create instant resentment. Finances have to be a team effort.

Structure a workable budget and do the monthly bill paying together. This helps relieve pressure from just one person and keeps both of you equally aware of your financial situation. Set short-term and long-term financial goals.

Consulting each other on any purchase over an agreed-upon amount is also very important. Choose a dollar amount ceiling that you can both agree upon.

Keep in mind that not all people have the same ideas about finances and upbringing can play a huge role.

I was raised in a single-parent household, very lower middle class. We lived paycheck to paycheck with no savings to fall back on. My mother never received child support and did not save for retirement. She worked her whole life and didn't stop working until she was too ill to work anymore.

I didn't learn the "you need to save for retirement" lesson until it was too late. Can you guess why?

A. No one told me to

B. My mother didn't model it

C. I'm an idiot and was almost forty before gaining employment with a retirement plan

D. All of the above

The correct answer is D, all of the above.

I won't refrain from telling anyone who will listen, to save for retirement.

Seriously, I can't stress this enough. So much so that I had my kids buy a savings type life insurance policy at age 18 and 19 respectively. If they continue to contribute $300.00 a month, they will be able to draw $67,777.00 a year at age 55 due to compound interest and stuff I don't understand.

I don't understand the process, but I do understand having the freedom and security to be able to retire. A retirement fund is paying yourself for your future. It's also never too early to start seeing a reputable financial planner.

Inheritance

What happens if you inherit money or property?

What happens if your partner inherits money or property?

Would it be yours?

Would it be his or hers?

Would it be considered ours?

Retirement

What does retirement look like?

Who asks that at 21? 27? 33? Smart people do, and here's a story to illustrate why.

True Story ~ *Green Acres*

City girl marries country boy (think of the television show *Green Acres*—Google this one).

City girl and country boy currently live in the city. He's a cop and she's a teacher. Perfect. Nice pensions already in place. He grew up in a small, rural, one-horse-town and knew deep down he wanted to retire in some Midwestern state on 200 acres.

This vision of their future, polarized their marriage. There were other issues too, but this one was the biggest. Twenty-two years later, it became apparent that their futures were not headed to the same place.

What does retirement feel like to you?

Relaxed?

Part-time job?

Volunteer work?

Traveling?

Be involved grandparents?

When do you retire?

. . .

Earliest opportunity?

Do you retire at the same time?

Why?

Do you move?

If so, how far from family?

Downsize residences?

Do you buy an RV and travel the states?

Be snowbirds and have two residences?

Do you have a senior/assisted living fund if you can't live alone any longer?

Do you assume your children will help you out when you get older?

Are you expecting a large inheritance?

. . .

Obviously, no one knows exactly what the future holds, but it helps to know you and your partner desire the same outcome. These future lifestyle choices can help keep your financial goals on track, especially if you are excited about what lies ahead.

What was your biggest takeaway from this chapter?

9

FIDELITY & HONESTY
SINNER OR SAINT?

Let's be real—everyone says they're going to be faithful—it's in the vows, right? There are so many examples of fidelity gone sideways that there could be a book about just that.

It comes down to two distinctions:

1. Faithful
2. Unfaithful

That's it. There is no in between. Either you are faithful to your partner or you are not. If you are religious, infidelity is a broken commandment. Pretty. Big. Deal.

Here are some very intimate questions to ask yourself and your partner:

Have you ever been unfaithful?

. . .

If you cheated in a previous relationship, should you tell your current partner?

If you tell them that you have been unfaithful in the past, do you fear they will judge you?

Is that "in the past" and you are not that same person?

Is that your pattern?

What do you feel compels someone to cheat?

Are any of these justifications acceptable for infidelity?

- The decision was made while under the influence
- It was just an opportunity
- It was an emotional affair
- It was just sex and it meant nothing
- Your partner had low self-esteem
- Your partner had a narcissistic personality
- It was "revenge sex" because your partner cheated

You can't be truly vulnerable if you're lying, and to be a cheater, you have to be a liar.

So, I have this friend...this is what I will say when referring to either myself, a friend, acquaintance, friend-of-a-friend, etc.

So, I have this friend, Betsy. At the very end of her very broken marriage, she was unfaithful because her husband had already cheated on her. Betsy sought out validation in the approval of the opposite sex.

If you find out your partner cheated in a past relationship, can you let that go and move forward in your relationship?

Or should you burn that furniture with an accelerant?
(Just a phrase! Do not burn any furniture, please.)

Here are some real-life stories that might inspire more questions and prompt you to determine what you would do if these situations happened to you. Names have been changed to protect the innocent.

Situation #1 ~ Not Enough Miles Away

So, I have this friend. Patty is on the verge of retirement and had been married for 30 long years when she finds out that her husband had been "doing" a married manicurist, 15 years his junior. Her husband Cliff begs her to stay and says he'll end the affair. Patty forgives him and she tries to move on with their newly retired lives. Cliff then goes back and forth between Patty and the manicurist, ultimately abandoning the marriage.

During this time, Patty's heart is shattered. Cliff couldn't stay away from his lover. Patty has a complete emotional breakdown and moves 3,000 miles to get away from Cliff.

To this day, Patty still doesn't know the reason he cheated. He never had the courage to be honest with her and tell her why. We secretly hope that the manicurist cheats and leaves Cliff for another man, soon.

Situation #2 ~ Karma

So, I have this friend. Monica is very religious and meets a man at work. Stan pretends to be a solid churchgoing, upstanding man. Stan also has a 14-year-old disabled son who requires diapering.

Monica and Stan go to church and life is good until they get married.

Stan loses his job and stays up late on the computer—playing "games" he says. He doesn't quit smoking like he said he would. Money is tight, but Monica keeps working, praying, and caring for his son.

A sound Christian, Monica won't divorce him.

Then, one day Stan drops dead. He apparently wasn't in the best of health. Unfortunately, "stuff" starts to shake out. Online porn, an online affair, and get this--Stan was giving the money Monica earned to his online girlfriend. Are you kidding me?

I think he should have suffered from syphilis first and then dropped dead.

Monica was scammed and used, but her situation ended up a case of pure Karma via prayer.

Situation #3 ~ Made for TV Movie

I have a friend. Dan and Jan, had been married for 18 years. They have 3 kids under 13 and a 20-year-old nanny. Yes, I said a 20-year-old nanny. Then 50-year-old-dad Dan has an affair with the 20-year-old nanny. When he finally gets caught, Dan leaves his wife and kids for the nanny. Talk about being the midlife crisis cliché.

So, you can probably guess what happened next. Daddy Dan is broke now, having acquired child support for 3 kids, spousal support and hair plugs. His 20-year-old nanny girlfriend disappeared just like his family, money, and his hair.

You might be thinking, there were probably other underlying marital issues. The real question is why didn't he have the courage to leave his wife first, before the affair? That is what's hard to understand. Correction, I do understand, it's the "having your cake and eating it too" mentality.

Situation #4 ~ Against the Odds

So, I have this friend. Nancy cheated on her husband for over two years before she left him. Her lover was married as well. They both continued their respective marriages for sake of their kids. Because they were both miserable in their marriages, the affair seemed like the answer to their mutual angst. Nancy finally left her husband, but it took her lover another year before he left his wife. Of course, this doesn't make it right.

Nancy terribly regrets the affair and wishes she would have ended her marriage before beginning a new relationship. The fallout from the affair still rears its ugly head now and then, but ten years later Nancy and her lover are still together.

Most couples believe they will be faithful when they get married. However, marriage can be challenging, people change, and instead of working through things or ending the relationship first, infidelity can happen.

You can try to weed out a "player", especially if you ask the right questions, keep your eyes and ears open, and think with your head as well as your heart. Be realistic about what a committed monogamous relationship involves. Reflect on your beliefs, cultivate positive relationship role models, and be true to your deal breakers.

Honesty

Lying undermines trust and trust is essential to a healthy, solid relationship. If your partner habitually lies, at some point it will come out. If they deceitfully lie, this ARF shouldn't be ignored or tolerated.

Here are some variations of lying.

The exaggeration lie = I sold my 1989 Volvo for $20,000. Impossible.
The "protect someone's feelings" lie = Someone asks if you like their new haircut. You say yes because you don't want to hurt their feelings.
The deceitful lie = I had to work late because of a deadline, when in reality they went to happy hour after work with a sexy new co-worker.

Sometimes people lie due to fear, insecurities, or other reasons. That doesn't always mean that the lie was intended to be malicious. If you catch your partner in a lie and they confess, is up to you to decide if you want to forgive and whether or not you can trust them moving forward.

If you catch your partner in a lie and they lie to get out of the lie, you may be dealing with ARF.

The best course of action is not to lie in the first place, then you have nothing to worry about.

What was your biggest takeaway from this chapter?

10

MENTAL HEALTH
LET'S TALK ABOUT IT

Mental health is still an unspoken relationship topic that needs to be outed. Mental illness should not be a taboo subject. Mental health is just that, health. A health issue is like anything else you might encounter, such as diabetes. Mental illness has symptoms and treatments. The treatments vary, from medication to therapy. Untreated or undiagnosed mental illness usually ends up being self-medicated with illegal drugs or alcohol. Statistics have shown that most addicts suffer some form of mental health issue in addition to their addiction.

> According to the Journal of American Medical Association (JAMA), **50%** of the people who have a <u>severe</u> mental condition also have a substance abuse problem. The JAMA also found that **37%** of alcoholics have a mental illness, as do 53 % of drug addicts. This statistic <u>doesn't include</u> those with mild to moderate mental illness.

There should be no shame in sharing your mental health history with someone who loves you. It's not fair to enter into a committed relationship and not disclose mental health as you would any other health issue. Whomever you are committed to should know if you are managing an illness, whether it is diabetes or depression.

True Story ~ Lost in the Desert

So, I have this friend. Susie was on anti-depression medication for over ten years and didn't tell her husband of five years. Her depression medication had slowly stopped working over a period of about six months. Susie began to self-medicate with alcohol, not really realizing that her medication wasn't functioning at the same level. Can you spell disaster?

Susie was becoming dependent on alcohol; her husband Vince watched his wife crumble and didn't know why. One day Susie drove to the desert, got lost for 24 hours and scared her family to death. It was then that Susie finally confessed she suffered from depression.

Vince was devastated on several levels.

First, why did she hide it from him? Second, why didn't she trust him? Third, he watched her suffer when maybe he could have helped. He felt hurt and she felt ashamed.

Suggestion: Be open when you feel connected enough to trust. If you share and the other person rejects you, it's their loss, next! There should be no judgement if you are honest and getting the help you need. Maybe you needed mental health help to get through a difficult period like the death of a loved one, or maybe you take medication every day. Either way, getting help when you need it doesn't make you weak. Reaching-out for help takes courage and strength, strength to acknowledge you might not be able to go it alone.

There are two types of mental health issues that you may want to consider running from. They are narcissism and psychopathic personalities. These types of disorders are like vampires in a relationship. They suck the life out of their partner.

Manipulative skills are a distinct trait of a narcissist that may ultimately claim your sanity. The psychopathic personality feels no empathy; therefore, they can't truly love or connect with others. Their needs are all that matters. This is a top-level ARF that should not be glossed over in any way. The U.S. National Library of Medicine describes these personality disorders below:

Narcissistic personality disorder is a mental condition in which a person has:
- An excessive sense of self-importance
- An extreme preoccupation with themselves
- A lack of empathy for others

A person with this disorder may:
- React to criticism with rage, shame, or humiliation
- Take advantage of other people to achieve his or her own goals
- Have excessive feelings of self-importance
- Exaggerate achievements and talents
- Be preoccupied with fantasies of success, power, beauty, intelligence, or ideal love
- Have unreasonable expectations of favorable treatment
- Need constant attention and admiration
- Disregard the feelings of others, and have little ability to feel empathy
- Have obsessive self-interest
- Pursue mainly selfish goals

Antisocial personality disorder is a mental condition in which a person has a long-term pattern of manipulating, exploiting, or violating the rights of others without any remorse. This behavior may cause problems in relationships or at work and is often criminal.

A person with antisocial personality disorder may:

- Be able to act witty and charming
- Be good at flattery and manipulating other people's emotions
- Break the law repeatedly
- Disregard the safety of self and others
- Have problems with substance abuse
- Lie, steal, and fight often
- Not show guilt or remorse
- Often be angry or arrogant

Trauma

Life's traumatic events can mold us and have varying effects depending on the individual and the event. We can repress traumatic memories, constantly relive them, or seek professional help to try and deal with them. For someone who has already experienced trauma, any new trauma can easily trigger old memories and create a recurring cycle. This cycle can bring old traumas to the surface over and over again, never allowing for healing. It's like constantly ripping a bandage off a wound.

Dealing with past traumas and moving forward is different for everyone. The first step is to acknowledge the trauma, then seek help to deal with it, and hopefully, move on. Help for Post Traumatic Stress Syndrome (PTSD) can include psychiatric counseling, psychological therapy, medication, hypnotherapy, acupuncture, exercise, meditation, aroma therapy, Eastern medicine, prayer, light therapy, pet therapy, visceral therapy, and more.

> **Post-traumatic stress disorder (PTSD)** is a mental health disorder that some people develop after they experience or see a traumatic event. The traumatic event may be life-threatening, such as combat, a natural disaster, a car accident, or sexual assault. But sometimes the event is not necessarily a dangerous one. For example, the sudden, unexpected death of a loved one can also cause PTSD.
>
> In time, most people recover from this naturally. But people with PTSD don't feel better. They feel stressed and frightened long after

the trauma is over. In some cases, the PTSD symptoms may start later on. They might also come and go over time. [1]

Military personnel and first responders are who most people think of when they hear the term PTSD, but trauma happens every day to everyday people. It happens to the person experiencing the trauma as well as those witnessing the trauma.

Getting a diagnosis of PTSD is the real question. If someone doesn't know they might have PTSD or doesn't understand the signs, symptoms, or behaviors, they aren't as likely to get help. The symptoms, severity, and frequency can vary from male to female, thus making a clear diagnosis sometimes difficult. This is especially difficult if the person is self-medicating with illegal drugs or alcohol.

Most people have experienced some sort of trauma by the time they are 18.

True Story ~ Bingo

So, I have this friend. Anne repressed childhood molestation until she was in her early thirties. Why did that memory surface after twenty years? No clue. Even after remembering the trauma, Anne told no one until she was forty. She was so ashamed. While seeing a counselor to deal with mother's impending death, she finally shared the trauma. The counselor looked at her like "bingo"!

Familiar with Anne's behavior patterns, the counselor could see Anne was suffering from PTSD.

Would you ask someone you love if they have mental health issues?

Do you want to know if they have these issues?

. . .

These are hard questions, but I say yes, you should ask, and yes, you should know.

Sharing your personal or family history of trauma can open the door to a conversation.

Try the following door-openers:

Do you have any health concerns?

Is there an experience you wish never happened?

Why?

Is there something you wish you had never witnessed?

Why?

If you can truly be open and vulnerable, your connection should deepen from knowing someone's hurts and why they might behave a certain way.

If you don't ask the really tough questions, you may never know the reasons behind someone's behaviors. Therefore, how can you make an educated decision or choice?

PTSD Hotline / Crisis Numbers
   Veteran Crisis Line
   1.800.273.TALK (8255) – Veterans Press '1
   National Veterans Foundation Hotline
   1.888.777.4443

Rape, Abuse, and Incest National Network (RAIN) (24 Hours)
1.800.656.4673
National Domestic Violence Hotline
1.800.799.7233

What was your biggest takeaway from this chapter?

11

ALCOHOL AND DRUG USE
BOTTOMS UP OR DOWN?

Without question, addiction can destroy a relationship the same way the Titanic was destroyed by hitting an iceberg. Addiction has no social or economic boundaries. Be real with yourself and hopefully your partner will be real too when you delve into this subject matter.

I'd like to think most people experiment with alcohol and can be responsible drinkers. But the reality is that millions are addicted to a legal substance, then add in the millions addicted to illegal drugs.

Do you think you have a drug or alcohol or addiction problem?

Do you think your partner has a problem?

When did you begin drinking or using drugs?

- Underage drinking?
- College Partying?

- Weekend binging?
- When did it end?
- Has it ended?

Was drinking or drug use a problem in the past?

If you don't have a problem, can you live with someone who has a substance abuse problem or is now in recovery?

If you are the one with the problem, can someone live with you?

If you both have addiction issues, will you feed off the other person's addiction to remain addicted?

If you are sober (or in recovery) and the other person isn't, then what?

Do you end the relationship?

If you both have a problem, will either of you agree to go get help and be sober?

Sometimes you don't initially see the addiction issue, or it can develop over time, which makes this topic so insidious. Addiction is also listed in chapter 25 as ARF.

Please be open and talk about past substance experimentation and current use. If you smoke pot every day before work, you have to be honest about that. Maybe that is your job, to test pot strains all day. Just kidding. Be open and lay it out.

Maybe try this approach:

Tell me about your memories in reference to alcohol or drugs?

For me, my earliest memories of alcohol would be of my mom. I remember jug-sized bottles of wine at home. I drank my first alcoholic beverage around sixteen. My friends and I would "fish" (ask someone of age to purchase) for alcohol at the liquor store. I'm still amazed that I am not an alcoholic. Somehow, I managed to sidestep that genetic bullet with my name on it.

Life Story ~ Walk of Shame

So, I have this friend. Her dad drank a lot and let her down more times that she could count. She swore to herself she would never be a slave to alcohol, and thankfully she isn't. She rarely has a glass of wine. The memories of her dad are filled with sadness and disappointment. Memories she wishes she could erase, like him stumbling home from the bar with a skanky tramp on his arm. Samantha's story could have easily gone the other way. She could have chosen alcohol to dull and drown out painful memories of her childhood.

Life Story ~ Down in His Cups

So, I have this friend. She married young and thought she had it all: a husband with an excellent job, a small house they owned, and a baby. However, her husband Paul didn't seem to want to "grow up" as she called it. Paul would go out after work and drink with the boys; he would stay up late at the neighbor's house drinking and then call in sick to work. Eventually, it cost him his job and family because he refused to admit he was an alcoholic and get the necessary help.

Most of the population has encountered someone with substance abuse.

How has substance abuse affected your life, if at all?

Do you know someone with an addiction?

How if at all, has this person's addiction affected your life?

Addiction can also include smoking of various types. Smoking cigarettes, cigars, hookahs, old school tobacco pipes, e-cigs or vape pipes. All of these have been proven to be addictive and a hard habit to break, not to mention that smoking is bad for your health.

Smoking:

Is smoking of any kind a deal breaker?

Could you deal with occasional smoking? (Like a cigar while golfing.)

Do you need to know if your partner was a previous smoker?

What if you are both smokers and then one of you quit?

Would the other person have to quit also?

Gambling:

Gambling is one of the oldest addictions.

Where do you stand on the topic of gambling?

Do you know someone who has a gambling problem?

Have you witnessed the effect gambling can take in a relationship, marriage, or family?

People steal, embezzle, and commit fraud for gambling money just like drug money.

If you or someone you know needs help, please reach out to these free resources:
    1-800-GAMBLER - Free, confidential help
    Cdph.ca.gov/ 1-800-426-2537
    Text 'Support' to 53342

What was your biggest takeaway from this chapter?

12

MANNERS, POLITENESS, & PATIENCE
ASK DEAR ABBY

Whether you are old-fashioned or a modern feminist, fundamental principles apply to manners and politeness. Where do you stand and what are your expectations for the following?

Opening doors?

- All the time?
- Sometimes?
- Never?

Pulling out chairs?

- All the time?
- Sometimes?
- Never?

Salutations and Introductions?

How do you address elders?

How do you want to be introduced?
   "I'd like you to meet the most recent person I am sleeping with."
   Just kidding.
   Table manners?
   Proper use of silverware?
   Napkin in lap?
   Elbows on the table?

At some point, we can tend to get comfortable with our partners and allow certain bodily functions to let go in front of each other.
   Do you want to keep some dignity while passing gas?
   Do you discuss your menstrual cycles in detail?
   Do you discuss your bowel movements?

Patience:

I feel that patience is a behavior to be observed and one of concern.
   Patience is an important piece of life. Our current world thrives on instant gratification. You can get almost anything with a tap of your fingers on a keyboard or smartphone.
   So, no need for patience, right? Wrong.
   Technology doesn't always work out the way you want it to. What about traffic, crowds, screaming children, dropped cell signals and long lines?
   It's these scenarios and more that require patience. Patience with

people in general and in your relationship is paramount. Everyone loses their cool from time to time. However, if someone can't handle waiting at a red light, experiencing a flight delay, or the slow checker at the grocery store without an outburst or disdain, are they going to be patient enough to listen to you, your side of an issue, or a concern?

Are they patient enough to soothe a teething baby who is inconsolable, without frustration or anger?

How patient is your partner when teaching you something new?

Is your partner patient while teaching?

Do they get frustrated with you, give up, or worse yet, make you feel incompetent?

How do you handle waiting in a long, crowded line?

How do you deal with red lights or getting cut off while driving?

How do you handle difficult situations with children and the elderly?

How do you deal with the infirm or unstable?

How do you handle someone interrupting you?

. . .

Are you on time?

Do you consistently run late?

A lack of patience can also signal a selfish or narcissistic personality. Some people won't have patience to hear you, they're too busy listening to themselves.

Pure patience is an art form just like active listening. The more you embrace the calm of patience the better you'll know that rushing, unless it is mandated or an emergency, is not a healthy way to live. Running late and rushing creates unnecessary stress, anxiety, and grief.

Allowing that one car to cut in front of you might change your arrival time by a minute or two. Tailgating the car in front of you so the other car can't squeeze into your lane as you swear at them is only hurting you. Impatience hurts your mental health, your blood pressure, your stress level and could possibly cost you your life.

It's just not worth it.

Just like impatience, being late takes a toll on you mentally and physically. Plan a ten-minute early buffer. With anything that requires a specific time of arrival like work, school, a flight, or an appointment, you need to allow yourself enough time to get ready, get others ready if necessary, and travel time.

When you are running late, the car in front of you is always driving too slowly, then you can't find a parking spot, and then the elevator is too slow, which in turn can make you lose your patience quickly.

You might also take unnecessary risks when running late like speeding which is never worth the risk. Take the extra early time to breathe, check your phone, look in the mirror and make sure you don't have something stuck in your teeth.

. . .

What was your biggest takeaway from this chapter?

13

FIGHTING STYLE
MMA OR WWF?

Learning your and your partner's fighting styles can assist in understanding reactions and resolving disagreements. Notice how your partner reacts when they are upset with you and how you react when you are upset with them.

Ask yourself and your partner the following:

Are you calm when expressing your concern or upset?

Do you defend yourself or actions?

Do you place blame?

Do you yell?

Name call?

. . .

Use profanity?

Do you blow up easily?

Do you ignore you partner?

Are you an argument avoider?

Do you shut down?

Do you criticize?

Bring up past events?

Do you reflect the same behavior?

Do you try to get to the bottom of the issue or brush it under the rug?

Do you or your partner always have to be right?

Does it take a lot to get you upset?

. . .

If yes, when you do finally get upset do you blowup?

Don't address the issue and agree to disagree?

Do you push down the anger for later resentment?

Do you cave in if your partner cries?

Do you threaten self-harm during a fight?

Do you have to keep the argument going until a resolution is found or can it be tabled for another time?

Do you try not to go to bed angry?

Do you find a resolution and move forward?

Getting through an argument, disagreement, or fight, is a relationship test. Please remember words can't be taken back once they have left your mouth, whether you truly meant them or not. Words can cut like a knife. Be aware of what you say, especially in the heat of the moment. Things said are like things seen. Once heard you can't unhear them.

Consider an eight-second rule before speaking.

Take eight seconds to decide if what you are about to say is helpful or harmful. This little tool can really make a huge difference in how you communicate during an argument. It works great in the workplace too.

The eight-second rule is a gem.

How you engage with each other during and after an argument can set a lasting tone. If one person is an avoider and the other person keeps the argument going until a resolution is found, it may push the avoider completely out of the relationship.

The avoider may have grown-up witnessing harsh fighting between their parents and does not want to repeat that cycle. It doesn't mean that they don't want to resolve the issue, but they might prefer to take a smoother, longer road at a later time when things have calmed down. Learning each other's style will help in finding a resolution without adding in more hurt feelings.

What was your biggest takeaway from this chapter?

14

DO YOU PRETZEL?
IT'S TIME TO UNTWIST

Generally, insecure people-pleasers, (like I used to be) tend to do what has been coined pretzeling. Pretzeling is when you contort yourself to fit the mold of the person you want or are with to their satisfaction and expectation. You adjust your opinions, thoughts, and feelings, to match the other person's. You change your appearance to their preferences. You squash down any feelings of hurt or anger for fear of rejection or criticism.

Being a pretzel is mentally, physically, and emotionally exhausting. Pretzels can manifest many real physical ailments like anxiety, ulcers, and cancer, by keeping up the contortion at the expense of their health.

Low self-worth also involves self-criticism and the inability to accept a sincere compliment. In lieu of a "thank you" for the compliment, it may be met with "not even," "no," or "I'm not."

A few signs of low self-esteem or insecurity:

- Overly self-critical
- Feeling unworthy, not good enough

- Rejecting compliments
- Unrealistic views of appearance or personality
- Self-abuse (eating disorders, cutting)

It took me too many years before I was able to own myself "as is." It was a huge realization for me to accept that not everyone is going to approve of or like me. It was quite liberating, but it is still a struggle at times to push down "pretzel" tendencies.

True Story ~ MO = Modus Operandi

So, I have this friend. Tina's modus operandi was to run. She would end all of her relationships first.

How can someone hurt her if she leaves them first? Logical, right? No. No intimacy can be truly built if there is no trust. Tina's self-esteem was very low, she was a pretzel. She never felt that the men she was with really loved her just for her. She never let her guard down, ever. It was exhausting watching her twist herself like an actress in a never-ending play. Sadly, Tina hasn't yet experienced the depth of real intimacy that comes from unconditional love because she allows fear to paralyze her. Know fear, no love.

There are thousands of resources available to help with the process of self-assuredness if you struggle with low self-esteem. Bottom line, you are the only person who can change those thoughts and feelings.

So, if you are a pretzel, soft, hard, or somewhere in between, please stop it and stop it now. Sure, we could all use some self-improvement and fine tuning. That is what personal growth and accountability are about. There is no reason to twist yourself into someone you think someone else wants. Being loved by a few "as is" is much better than trying to be loved by all in pretzel mode.

What was your biggest takeaway from this chapter?

15

FRIENDS
I'LL BE THERE FOR YOU

Friends can play a pivotal role in your life and in your relationships. Good friends applaud you, support you, and sometimes tell you what you might not want to hear. That is how you know they are good friends. A true friend will hold your confidence and never judge or betray you. Good friends have your best interests at heart.

Analyze your friendships.

Analyze yourself as a friend.

What do you value most in a friendship?

How do you know someone is a good friend?

- Trust?
- Loyalty?
- Do they judge you or others?
- Do you feel safe confiding in them?

- Know they have your back?
- Be your alibi?
- Hide the body? Just kidding.

Do you have enough friend time?

Does your partner support you when you spend time with your friends, or do they become jealous or passive aggressive?

Example: "Sure honey, go to happy hour with your friends after work and have fun," your partner says. But the whole time you are out they are blowing up your phone with snarky comments and accusations.

You or your partner may need more friend time than the other. It's wise to discuss the amount of time spent with friends and boundaries. If your partner is secure and wants what is best for you, they will want you to have time with the friends you love, just as you would want for them.

If your best friend sees or feels something isn't quite right (ARF) with your new love, don't be so quick to dismiss it, make excuses, or explain it away. Your friend probably sees what you can't because you are wearing "denial goggles."

Ask yourself and your partner these friend questions:

Do you like your partner's friends?

Do your partner's friends like you?

. . .

Do your friends like your partner?

Do you like all but one of their friends?

Do your friends think your partner is all wrong for you?

Do you tolerate your partner's friends out of obligation?

Would your friends tell you if they saw something suspicious about your partner?

Would you tell your partner your concerns about their choice of friends?

Do you go along with your friends or lead the crowd?

Do you balance friend time and relationship time?

Does a night out with friends take priority over your relationship?

Does your partner treat their friends better than you?

Do you ditch your friends when you are in a relationship?

. . .

Do you have "couple" friends?

If you don't have couple friends, you may want to develop those friendships. Couple friends can be a great source of support during difficult times in a relationship. They can provide a buffer and offer a safe zone for you and your partner.

Your partner should be your best friend or at least an equal to your best friend. That friend piece in your partnership lends support and encouragement like any best friend should. They are your cheering section. Part of being a couple is working towards mutual goals and dreams together like building a career, buying a home, or starting a family.

How do you want your individual goals or dreams supported?

Having your partner support you is critical, whether you are getting your Master's degree or opening your dream restaurant. Your dreams may be drastically different, but each person needs validation.

Does your partner help you reach for your dreams/goals?

Do they ask how can we make this happen?

Do they genuinely support you?

Do they offer encouragement?

. . .

Do they stop you from giving up?

When thinking about a lifetime relationship, whether it's love or friendship, having someone believe in you, encourage you, and have your back is vital. It defines what it is to be a real friend or partner. Your life partner should be your biggest fan. Yes, that's cheesy, but it's true.

What was your biggest takeaway from this chapter?

Before we get to the next two topics remember what everyone says: Don't talk religion or politics at a party. Well guess what, your relationship is not a party, and these two topics can be deal breakers for some people or can add cement to a relationship.

16

RELIGION AND POLITICS
A NO-NO AT PARTIES

Many people consider religious views before even dating someone. For example, a devout Christian might find it very difficult to date an atheist. Religion can be a deal breaker. Religion and faith are supposed to be symbols of peace and love, but they can create conflict if your beliefs are measurably different.

Do you need your beliefs to match up?

Do you believe in God or a higher power/source?

Are you spiritual?

Are you agonistic?

. . .

Are you an atheist?

What is your religion if you have one?

Do you believe in God, but not in organized religion?

Are you practicing your religion?

Was religion a childhood thing?

Have you converted or changed religions? If yes, why?

Would you convert religions for a relationship or marriage?

Are your core beliefs the same or different?

Will religion play a large role in your relationship?

If you and your partner have different religions (ex: Mormon and Jewish) can you blend?

Do you belong or have you belonged to a cult?

. . .

Some religions won't even consider blending for marriage. Wherever your beliefs lie, it is the conviction and strength behind them that will ultimately decide how important these questions will apply.

This can also apply to politics. Some people will not consider being with someone who doesn't share their political values or agenda. What is the most media-covered topic? Politics. Introduce your rightwing great grandpa who served in WWII to your bleeding-heart liberal feminist best friend and watch the sparks fly!

Depending on individual beliefs and roots, politics can be a dividing line like the North and South in *Gone with the Wind*.

Are politics important to you?

Where do you swing?

Right?

Left?

In the middle?

Green Party?

No affiliation at all?

Do you need your partner to share the same political viewpoint as you?

. . .

If not, can you agree to disagree regarding politics?

Did you assume a parent's political party?

Did you rebel and go against the family norm?

Are you an activist?

Do you vote?

Are you patriotic?

Do you believe in "conspiracy theories"?

Are political views or beliefs deal breakers?

The topics of religion and politics leave me stymied as both can be polarizing or a non-entity depending on the couple. Some of the most animated and entertaining after-dinner conversations I've listened to have featured religion and politics.

What was your biggest takeaway from this chapter?

17

SEX
BASIC INSTINCT

This chapter's questions are quite personal in nature. Consider when and how you ask your partner. These questions can help you create your love and deal breaker lists and find answers prior to making a life-altering commitment. You should be comfortable discussing intimacy if your relationship is emotionally mature and shares mutual trust.

The three little letters in the word sex should equal energy, instinct and survival.

Stop here. SLOW down.

Think...

What are you seeking?

A one night stand?

Short-term sexual encounters?

. . .

Monogamy?

A long-term committed relationship?

Marriage?

How long do you wait before having sex?

- One date?
- Three dates?
- Six weeks?
- Months?
- Years?
- Five minutes?
- After marriage?

How long you wait can be determined by what type of relationship you are seeking. If you are seeking a long-term relationship or marriage, you should consider waiting. Waiting on the physical piece until you've established monogamy helps build a foundation. Your chemistry might be off the charts, but if you rush in with just chemistry alone, your relationship can lack a solid foundation that comes from deeply knowing someone.

Introducing intimacy should be valued and can solidify your relationship with proper timing.

The following questions and answers could vary immensely from person to person depending on where they are at a particular time or age in their life.

How do you define sex?

- Is sex the act of intercourse itself?
- Oral sex?
- Manual stimulation?
- Anal sex?
- Internet, video, phone sex?
- All of the above?

There are many reasons why people might engage in sex relations quickly:

- Insecure or feelings of unworthiness
- Just dumped
- Seeking revenge sex
- Loneliness or neediness
- Wants to control or dominate
- A people pleaser or pretzel
- Possibly unstable

Why rush?

If you want a committed relationship, sex should come after monogamy, a mutually exclusive relationship. This should take time...there should be no rush in getting to know someone you may ultimately be having sex with the rest of your life.

The emotional bonding generally comes much faster for a woman after her first sexual encounter with a partner. Even if she mentally tries to separate herself and tries to acknowledge it as casual, her chemistry may still kick in and try to bond. Her heart may already be racing in the afterglow and her mind dreaming of her wedding dress.

. . .

What are you and your partner's expectations regarding sex? (Chapter 9 also covers the topic of expectations.)

Frequency:

How often do you have sex?

Every day?

Once a week?

Once a month?

Once a year?

Lights on?

Lights off?

Morning?

Noon?

Night?

. . .

Who should initiate sex?

- You?
- Your partner?
- Both?

Is your sex scheduled?

Do you have to be right-out-of-the-shower clean?

Mandatory foreplay?

Romantic sex with music and candles?

Make out session or kissing prior to sex?

Are drugs or alcohol involved or required for sex? (altered state) If yes? Why?

Public places?

Groomed?

Lingerie?

. . .

Sexy notes or texting, flirting?

Surprises?

Show up naked under a trench coat?

Group sex?

Role playing?

Fantasies?

Sex toys or aides?

Sexual enhancement medications?

S & M, bondage, domination?

Swingers' circles?

Great Sex

What do you need to make sex great for you?

Monogamy?

Have an emotional connection?

Must be in love?

Marriage?

Pure physical chemistry? (Rip your clothes off STAT)

Birth Control:

Who's responsible?

Him?

Her?

Both?

Sexually Transmitted Diseases (STDs):

If you have an STD that can't be cured like herpes/AIDS, do you tell?

When do you tell?

Before sex?

After sex?

If you are serial dating (having sex with multiple partners) do you tell your partners before sex that you are serial dating?

Pornography:

What do *you* define as pornography?

Playboy?

Hardcore rated XXX magazines, movies, websites?

S & M, bondage?

Where do *you* stand on pornography?

- Hell no.
- Yes, for him?

- Yes, for her?
- Yes, for both?
- Yes, if together only?

Strip Clubs:

Where do *you* stand on strip clubs?

Hell no! Over my dead body.

Sure, no problem.

Sure, if it's a special occasion like bachelor/bachelorette party.

Sure, if we go together.

Sex Stores:

Sure, let's go together and buy a new sex toy.

No, never.

Something that is done individually?

Intimacy is the key that can hinge or unhinge a relationship. Knowing your partner's view of sex is just another way to build a closer bond.

The previous questions may have been easy for you or awkward to answer. Either way you are learning and defining your thoughts and feelings regarding the questions posed and that is a good thing. Knowledge is power.

Sexual History:

Sexual history can be a scorcher to discuss, own, or acknowledge.

Men – Their pasts can be sordid and extensive without judgment.

Ladies – If you have had more than a handful of partners, you might be judged.

Why this mentality still applies in the 21st century blows my mind.

Nonetheless, a percentage of men still want to have sex with woman of "experience" but marry a virgin.

True Story ~ I'm Not a Slut

So, I have this friend. When she was pressed for an answer about her sexual past she lied, knowing enough about her man to know it would not bode well if she spilled the actual number of past sexual partners. Mary Ann wanted approval. Let's not forget she was in love. So, she says a number she thinks he wants to hear. And you might be thinking, why lie?

She felt justified in lying and here is why:

- Double standard bull$*&%
- Her sexual past is her business
- She is healthy and disease free

Mary Ann was not promiscuous, but she had experience, the kind of experience that made her a good lover. This usually takes some experimenting to achieve.

Men should appreciate a woman who has had enough partners to:

A. know what she wants and needs,

B. and know how to take care of his wants and needs.

Here are some choices if someone actually asks you how many partners you've had:

1. Avoid this topic
2. Be an actual virgin
3. Lie
4. Take the actual number of sexual partners you have had and divide by 10; that's the number you use
5. Tell the truth

There are few things that don't warrant full disclosure. This may be one of them, as long as you are not impacting the health of someone or creating a barrier in your relationship due to unresolved past traumas. It's a very personal choice to reveal this part of your past. You must be comfortable and authentic to whatever you decide in response to the question of sexual partner history.

Sexual Abuse:

If you have been abused, do you tell?

If yes, when do you tell?

Do you tell the story with details or just that it happened?

Having been sexually abused as a child or as adult can scar you for life. Your trust is destroyed. Fear can course through your veins and you may live in panic mode. You might even blame yourself.

If you have experienced any sexual abuse, please seek qualified professional help via psychiatry, counseling, support groups, meetings, or whatever you need to help you move through the trauma. Please don't go it alone. It is too hard to cope without help. You are not at fault. Most importantly, please don't try to make any feelings of pain, shame, guilt, or fear go away with substance abuse; it just makes things worse.

Resources:
   https://www.acf.hhs.gov › trauma-toolkit › victims-of-sexual-abuse
   https://www.rainn.org › articles › adult-survivors-child-sexual-abuse

What was your biggest takeaway from this chapter?

18

LAWLESS
BRUSHES WITH THE LAW

The punishment for breaking the law is usually how we decide what side we would rather be on.

Do you want to be in a relationship with someone who is in prison or running from the law?

If you ask your partner questions and don't feel the answers were honest, trust your gut and run a background check or check public records.

We live in the age of technology, use it.

Did you find or do you have:

An overdue library book?

Unpaid parking tickets?

. . .

Graffiti?

Shoplifted hemorrhoid cream because you were too embarrassed to buy it?

If you've been a halo-wearing angel, then the next questions won't apply to you. But, if you had any brushes with the law, then answer the following about the nature and severity of the crime:

Public urination?

Stole the school mascot?

Stole cigarettes, alcohol?

Driving Under the Influence (DUI)?

Breaking and entering?

Theft?

Stealing to feed an addiction (drugs, alcohol, gambling)?

Car theft?

. . .

Fraud, white collar crimes?

Crimes involving violence?

Are you on parole? If yes, for how long and what for?

What were your "crimes"?

Have you spent extended periods of time incarcerated?

Can you forgive a criminal past?

Real Situation ~ Popped

So, I have this friend. Lucy was the queen of shoplifting in high school. She stole just to see if she could pull it off. When she finally got "popped," it was the worst situation ever. Lucy was staying at her grandparents' house for the weekend, she went shoplifting at the neighborhood grocery store, and finally got caught. The undercover officer drove Lucy to her grandparents' house after searching her purse and finding money in it, money that her grandparents had given her. Her grandfather was in the military during WWII and had a serious heart condition. The look on her grandfather's face was first mortified, then deeply disgusted. It was forever etched into her memory. It was one of the hardest lessons she learned, and she broke her ailing grandfather's heart in the process.

Real Situation ~ Two is Not Better than One

So, I have this friend. Jake had 2 DUIs by the time he was 25. He said he was unlucky and that the two times he was arrested were the only times he'd ever driven under the influence. Huh? What? Who is high now? He must be high if he thinks anyone would believe that. But, then again, someone might believe him if they have "denial goggles" on. See chapter 25 on red flags.

Real Situation ~ Not a Pot of Gold

So, I have this friend. Ian sold weed in high school long before it was legal. During that time, he was the cool kid because he had money and weed. Guess what? High school doesn't last forever. Ian apparently thought he could sell pot for a living. After high school Ian kept dealing, but he now had rent and bills to pay since his parents kicked him out. While Ian was making larger and larger deals, he was also being tracked by the law. The law was patient and waited to bust him when he made his largest deal of all. That deal turned out to be a felony distribution bust in which he was sentenced to twelve years.

Laws and rules are set in place to protect the general public and circumvent anarchy. A life filled with arrests, court appearances, jail time, prison, and parole are a front row ticket ARF that will cause nothing but grief and heartache. Take off the "denial goggles" and look good-and-hard before attaching yourself to a partner whose life is littered with poor choices and chaos.

What was your biggest takeaway from this chapter?

19

LIVE TOGETHER
GO ALL IN OR WAIT TILL MARRIAGE?

Living together on a day-to-day basis is when you truly find out someone's level of cleanliness. Of course, you can certainly tell by visiting to see how their living space is managed. At that point, you might consider if their type of living environment is one you can adapt to or if you are willing to pick up the slack. In other words, if you are tidy and clean and your prospective partner is unorganized, you can consider one of the following:

1. Learn to live in disarray and let it go.
2. Be willing to pick up and organize for them without resentment.
3. Be a nag and get bitter.
4. End the relationship.

Living together makes sense on many levels. You can figure out each other's needs, wants, and habits in depth, 24-hour-a-day depth, observing each other at your best and worst. It also allows for an easier getaway if things get tough.

Although a marriage certificate is just a piece of paper to some, it does seem to make couples try much harder to work things out rather than ending a relationship that has no formal bond.

True Story ~ Delete, Delete, Delete!

So, I have this friend. Lily had been married before and wanted to set a good example for her kids; therefore, she didn't want to live with her partner before marriage. A month into her marriage she downloaded all her pictures, music, and documents onto her new husband Phil's computer since hers was old and they were combining households.

While searching for some of her photos, Lily found photos that absolutely should have been deleted by her new husband (with whom she was involved for two years prior to marriage). But there the photos were in all their glory. So, you're thinking, "So what? He was single before you." The thing is these items were saved during the time their relationship was exclusive and later engaged. She subsequently asked to access his email; he agreed, and it was bad.

Lily's trust was shattered. Although there was no proof of physical infidelity, she could not shake the feeling of distrust. Lily would never have married Phil if she had been privy to what was on the computer sooner.

It would have been ARF she would not have ignored.

True Story ~ Cleaning Up

So, I have this friend. Bill fell head over heels in love with a woman and they decide to buy a house during their engagement. His fiancée had a successful house-cleaning business, but she can't be on the loan due to a previous credit issue. No worries, Bill makes enough to buy the house on his own. He trusts his fiancée and is in love. While unpacking Bill opens a backpack he thought was his (same color, size, etc.) What do you think was inside?

You're right if you guessed illegal drugs. Her "cleaning business" was cleaning up in the drug trade. Let's just say it was a tricky situation. He sold the house and is now single.

Tricky, as he had to remove himself from the relationship and get her to move out. But, slightly less of a nightmare as they were not yet married. Bill didn't have a standard ARF, but he could have asked more questions and dug deeper into her business since she had credit issues.

Even if she lied to him, at least he would have tried.

This leads to the privacy topic as you and your partner had lives and experiences prior to your relationship.

What do you consider private in a relationship?

Should there be things kept secret, things just for you?

What should you do with letters, cards, and photos from past relationships?

- Keep?
- Toss?
- Show and tell?
- What about physical space and privacy?

Do you have an "enter anytime" policy for the bathroom?

Do you need alone time to construct your face, hair, make-up?

Is there any mystery left in the bathroom?

. . .

What about alone/private time to:

- Meditate
- Pray or have religious rituals
- Yoga
- Walk
- Read
- Create
- Write or journal
- Watch different shows or movies
- Take a trip

Time alone is important to maintain balance in yourself and in your relationship.

What was your biggest takeaway from this chapter?

20

MARRIAGE, IN-LAWS, & FAMILY
TILL DEATH DO US PART

When you visualize the type of marriage and home life you want to embrace, think of the personality traits, behaviors, and relationship models that you want to experience.

Mature relationships take time.

Personal growth, along with a couple's growth, communication skills, mutual respect, and realistic expectations are the building blocks. Patience is mandatory to work through life together as one unit.

Is marriage a must have for you?

Would you be satisfied with just living together?

How long before the topic of marriage is brought up?

. . .

During the first date?

After a year of dating?

After five years of dating?

Once you are exclusive or monogamous?

After you've said, "I love you"?

Does it matter who brings up the topic of marriage?

Is it gender specific?

Do you need your family's approval before marriage?

Do you want your partner to ask your parents' permission before proposing?

If the woman brings up marriage first, will the man run like his hair is on fire?

If the man brings up marriage too soon, will the woman think he's desperate?

. . .

Do you want or need a formal proposal?

How long would you wait for a proposal?

A year, two years, forever?

Would you leave a relationship if it isn't headed towards marriage?

How long do you want to be engaged?

A year, two years, five days?

Vegas wedding baby!

Do you need a church wedding?

Do you have to be married before you have sex?

Do you have to be married before you have children?

What does marriage look like to you? Is it very traditional with conservative gender roles? Is it liberal?

Are you flexible and unconventional? Moderate balance of both?

. . .

Does just the husband work?

Just the wife work?

Both work?

Both work until you have kids?

Don't work conventional jobs and join the Peace Corps?

Who cooks?

Who cleans?

Who shops?

Are these shared duties?

50/50 split?

Do you seek pre-martial counseling?

. . .

Marriage is supposed to be forever, but as statistics show it's a fifty-fifty crap shoot. Marriage can be such a source of joy, but it isn't always easy, and it's not supposed to end.

No one enters into their marriage thinking it will end in divorce. It's inconceivable that we or the person we have chosen will ever change, fall out of love, or do anything to warrant a divorce.

However, the statistics say otherwise:

> Current divorce rate in American 2019 is 50% of married couples end in divorce. However, marriages are also good for children; growing up in a happy home protects children from mental, physical, educational and social problems. However, about 40 to 50 percent of married couples in the United States divorce. The divorce rate for subsequent marriages is even higher.[1]

Repeating a pattern of choosing the same type of partner with the same dysfunctions or emotional issues is relatively common from first to third marriages. Self-awareness, accountability, and good therapy can help someone avoid repeating a pattern of negative choices.

Another issue is when newly divorced people don't take enough time to deal with the pain of the split, the loss of the marriage, and truly heal. The recovery process after divorce has been the topic of hundreds of books. Instead of taking the needed time to recover, some may enter a rebound relationship. In addition, some people are so afraid of being alone they will stay in an unhealthy relationship. Learning to be alone can be paramount in learning about yourself as well as what you may or may not want in your next partner, like deal breakers.

Why is there such a deep culture of "divorce shaming" when approximately half of all marriages end in divorce? It takes an enormous amount of courage to risk your heart again for a second, third or whatever time. If a marriage fails it doesn't mean the couple should be shamed for the demise of their marriage. Ideally, they should take the needed time to evaluate, analyze, and reflect on what went wrong and why, and then address any shortcomings and make positive changes. No one should be predestined to live in a loveless, abusive, or dysfunctional marriage for fear of "divorce shaming."

So, I have this friend. Rachel met her first husband at nineteen and married at twenty-one. He was the "life" of the party, then that "life" fell into alcoholism. Marriage number one ended, leaving her with two small children. She then rebounded into marriage number two, marrying a man with whom she already knew and trusted. He was seven-years sober when they married. He fell off the wagon multiple times which led to divorce number two. Six years later, her third marriage was to a man who had to be drug tested for work. She thought that was the safe choice. However, she was wearing "denial goggles" in regard to his level of alcohol consumption.

She had unwittingly chosen three addictive personalities without addressing the common denominator in all these marriages, which was her. Breaking her negative choosing pattern took awareness, accountability, and self-acceptance for her decisions.

I know couples who sleep in separate bedrooms for years, live like roommates, and want to stab each other in the neck with a steak knife. (Just kidding about the steak knife.)

So, if you have been divorce-shamed, let it go. Maybe your lessons make you a better partner or lover. Why would it be considered shameful to try again?

Not everyone gets the first marriage that lasts forever. Some do, some don't. But no one on earth gets to judge, ever.

Would you stay in a marriage just for the sake of the vows?

Is there an acceptable reason for divorce?

Do you think divorce is shameful?

. . .

Do you think less of your divorced friends or family?

If you live with someone for ten years without being married and then break up is that any different than the end of a ten-year marriage?

Do you think that all avenues should be explored before divorcing?

Remember that your upbringing, role models, and expectations play a large role in who we marry and why we divorce. Some people have solid foundations to start with and others have cracked ones.

Bottom line: we are all human and worthy to give love and be loved.

The questions in this book are to help you find out more about yourself and your partner so you can make educated decisions and hammer out possible snags before they cause heartache.

In-Laws and Family

This topic typically doesn't get enough airtime prior to a serious committed relationship or marriage.

Let's Start with Boundaries:

How do you feel about family visits?

How long?

A day, a weekend, a week, two weeks?

. . .

How often?

Do they visit once a month, once a year?

Who's allowed to visit?

Parents, siblings, aunts, uncles, with all their kids and the dog?

When? Holidays, summertime?

Who pays? Who covers costs of flights if needed, food, entertainment, meals out?

Where do they stay?

Hotel?

Your house?

Can your crazy-black-sheep uncle come for the summer, sleep on the couch, and bring his Mastiff?

In-laws / Parents:

Do they have a say in your marriage?

. . .

Do they have to call before coming over, or is it a drop-in whenever situation?

Do they have a say in how you and your partner raise your kids?

Is it ever all right to ban an in-law or parent from visiting or having contact with your children (safety, alcohol, abuse, etc.)?

If yes, why?

Ex-spouse and Ex-family:

Do you remain in close contact with your ex or ex's family members?

Why?

If you have children (until age eighteen) there is usually necessary communication between ex-spouses.

Contact with ex only because of joint custody of children?

Text messages?

Email?

Do you have any contact with an ex?

. . .

If yes, why?

No contact – cut all ties?

What is considered appropriate contact?

Holidays:

Whose house are you celebrating at?

When?

Why?

Expectations?

Split visits?

Rotate visits?

One year at mom's and next year at dad's?

Extended family vacations?

Family Closeness:

Are you a part of a close-knit family?

Do you see family frequently?

Are unannounced visits acceptable?

Do you bail family out of mishaps?

What's the family culture (special holidays, family size, etc.)?

Do you see family only on birthdays and holidays?

Do you talk every day to a specific family member?

Can you adapt to different family dynamics?

Can you make compromises where your partner's family is concerned?

In-laws and family can and should be a great source of pride, happiness, and support. As the old saying goes, "Blood is thicker than water." Your family should be bedrock on which to lay your weary head, celebrate life's milestones and holidays, and help you through difficult times. However, we don't get to choose our family; instead, they are given to us like a birthmark. This being said, you also get to choose once you are of a certain age, if you want to continue a relationship with your family members.

Choice can be a beautiful thing.

What was your biggest takeaway from this chapter?

21

CHILDREN
BLESSED EVENT

Seems like such an easy yes or no question, right? Yes, you want kids, or no, you don't. Or, if your partner says no now, do you think they will change their mind at a later date?

Just agreeing on yes or no seems like a no-brainer question, but let's go a little deeper before you decide to procreate with someone.

Children are the greatest gift. Creating a life and being responsible for that life, for a minimum of 18 years, takes commitment and grit. You are responsible for creating your children's very existence, maintaining their entire physical and mental health, loving them, providing for them, teaching them, giving guidance, setting boundaries, being a role model, and watching their every movement to keep them safe, 24 hours a day, 7 days a week, 365 days a year.

Giving them never-ending, unconditional love, from the second you and your partner know you're pregnant, requires dedication.

Can you do it?

. . .

ALL of it?

Are you procreating for the right reasons?

Is having children what you want or a family expectation?

Are you having a child to make someone else happy?

When do you decide to become pregnant?

Plan it out?

Let it happen?

How long do you try before you give up?

Do you give up?

Do you try alternative ways to become pregnant?

Consider a surrogate?

Are you willing to adopt?

Parenting:

What are the parenting expectations going to be?

It is 50/50 split?

Old school, mother-centered diaper duty?

Will one of the two parents stay home and raise children?

If so, which parent?

If not, who will care for your children while both parents work?

Daycare center? In-home babysitting? Nanny? Family members?

Typically, you believe your relationship will last forever when you decide to have a child. Or maybe you're thinking, if I get pregnant, then he will love me and commit to a relationship. Back in the day, we called this "trapping the man." Well, guess what, women still do this today and will continue to do this.

Women have the power to procreate without the man's consent. The reverse is to be raped. It then would not be a woman's choice to become pregnant. However, depending on where you live in this world, women also have the legal choice to remain pregnant or not.

What all children truly need is unconditional love, attention, patience, protection, guidance, and support. Guide them and be the parent, not the friend. (That never works well – especially when kids hit middle school.) Children want parents. They can get their own friends.

What was your biggest takeaway from this chapter?

22
HOUSEHOLD DYNAMICS
WHO WAS IN YOUR HOUSE?

As a child, your typical first impression of a household is usually your own. The parental household dynamic effects the relationship role-model overall. Maybe you had the nuclear household with a mom and a dad or one of several other variations.

What was your household dynamic:

Nuclear household with one dad and one mom?

Stepparent?

Was it a split household between two parents?

Single parent household?

. . .

Did you have grandparents for parents?

Raised by other family members – aunt and uncle?

Foster parents?

Same-sex parents?

My mother was a single-parent. I was in daycare as a small child, after-school care until 5th grade, then a latchkey child (home alone). That lifestyle made me independent, but I also longed for siblings.

Did your home dynamic stay the same throughout your childhood?

If your household dynamic changed, what age were you and why?

Did you gain siblings or did your parents divorce?

If you could go back and change your childhood household dynamic, what would you have wanted? Why?

As an only child I became very responsible and accustomed to being alone. I was determined not to repeat the "only child" pattern when it came time to have kids of my own. Two kids were a minimum.
    Parenting choices have an everlasting effect. The first five years are vital to a child's emotional health, self-worth, developmental

growth, and ability to bond, learn right from wrong, and establishing boundaries. Being a parent is a full-time job giving unconditional love, having unlimited patience, setting boundaries, following through, and being the bad guy even when you don't want to be.

What was your family's parenting style?

- Strict?
- Fair?
- Hippie status?
- Laid-back?
- Pushovers?
- Lazy?
- Loving?
- Supportive?
- Over-involved?
- Uninvolved?
- Critical?
- Selfless?
- Spoiled you?
- Selfish?
- Self-involved?
- High expectations?
- Too much pressure?
- Overbearing?
- Overprotective?
- Inattentive?
- Alcoholic/drug addict?
- Mentally unstable?
- Physically disabled?
- Long-term illness?

Did your parents try to live their unfilled dreams through you as a child?

LEAH KAY ROSSI

. . .

Were you pushed into sports or music?

Did your parents <u>do</u> everything for you?

Did your parents <u>buy</u> everything for you?

What types of boundaries did you have, if any?

- Meals?
- Bedtimes?
- Chores?

What was the discipline style you had growing up?

Were you spanked as a child?

Did you have "time-outs?"

Were you grounded or made to stay home after you got into trouble?

Did your parents take away toys or privileges as punishment?

Do you have sense of entitlement?

. . .

Did you parents make excuses for your poor behavior?

Who taught you about morals and ethics?

Who taught you about social and emotional behaviors, like empathy?

- Relatives?
- Friends?
- Church?
- School?
- Social Media?
- Movies?
- Music artists or sports idols?

My mother's mother never talked to her about men, relationships, love, sex, birth control, alcohol, or money, and my mother never talked to me. I broke that cycle with my own kids with age-appropriate information and communication.

As Dr. Pepper Schwartz so appropriately stated, "Parents aren't sex education experts just because they are parents."

Blending Families:

Blending and co-mingling of children has to be one of the hardest pieces when re-marrying. Just because you love your spouse doesn't mean your kids will. There could be a million reasons why not, but it doesn't matter. Kids have their own thoughts and feelings; therefore, blending a family is one of the top reasons to get family counseling.

. . .

Dating someone with children is entirely different than living with that person with your children and their children. These blending family questions below should be discussed honestly and in depth.

Are you capable of blending?

Treat stepchildren equally?

Not compare?

What are the expectations as a stepparent?

What are the parenting styles of each parent in the child's life?

What comes first in the household?

Marriage or kids?

Ages of the children seems to play a huge role in blending.

- < 5 – generally easier for the children and parents to adapt.
- 6-10 is a little more difficult to adapt – kids can struggle with having two sets of parents, two households with different expectations.
- 11-17 is the hardest – these kids can tend to blame the new spouse/stepparent and might not want to interact in a parent/child relationship with them. They feel too old for

parent/child interaction and feel they already have a mother or father of their own.

If you already have kids and a parenting style, is it similar to your partner's?

How do you praise your kids?

How do you set boundaries?

How do you set expectations?

How do you discipline?

Your kids?

Your partner's kids?

All the kids?

Individually?

Discipline your own kids only?

. . .

Are you/your partner in sync?

These are just some basic questions and concerns when blending a family that should be discussed. Verbal agreements can be easily forgotten. Putting an agreed-upon parenting plan with clear expectations in writing is a great place to refer to if needed. It can help to clarify and ground a situation. Nothing is set in stone unless you both agree upon it and plan to adhere to it.

Life brings constant change and sometimes plans need adjusting. Creating a solid foundation of expectations can really help with structure and the task of co-parenting in a blended family. An excellent family counselor can help facilitate this process.

True Story ~ Teenage Stepchildren

So, I have this friend. Julie has three boys. Her future husband Steve has two daughters and one son. From the beginning there were issues. His girls were unwelcoming and verbalized how they disliked Julie, but his son had no issue with her. Steve's daughter's barely acknowledged Julie's presence.

Julie's ARF was the girl's behavior. She was in love with Steve and kept telling herself the girls would warm up to her. Julie never had an issue before with anyone's kids not liking her. The thing is it wasn't Julie.

To clarify, see Julie's choices below. ARF is the thing you choose to ignore now and regret later. The following five responses are what we tell ourselves to justify the red flag behavior.

1. The behavior or trait will go away
2. They will change
3. They will change for me
4. I can change or fix them
5. Stay in complete denial (my personal favorite)

Julie married and sadly, she was wrong. Instead of sharing her concerns about Steve's daughters she squashed her feelings for fear he would dump her if she pushed the issue. This was an unfortunate mistake. They could have opened conversations that might have helped and hopefully created a path to understanding for all involved.

What was your biggest takeaway from this chapter?

23

PETS
FUR OR NO FUR?

Pets are a large part of American culture. Pets offer unconditional companionship. However, pets require time, attention, and care. They are dependent on their owners like a child is to their parents. How someone cares for their pet can say a lot about them.

How do you feel about pets?

Are pets a must have?
　No way?
　Can have, but not mandatory and can do without?

Allergic? To what animal?

Do you have a pet?

What kind of pet?

Do you spend enough time with the pet?

Walking it?

Training it?

Grooming it?

Do you keep its living space clean?

Do you treat the pet like family?

Does the pet take the place of a child?

Are you obsessive with your pet and take it everywhere?

If so, what need is the pet providing?

Does the pet come before your partner?

. . .

Where does the pet sleep?

Would you get rid of a pet if your partner was severely allergic?

Pets provide pure unconditional love and are proven to add years to your life span. But remember that pets can't change adult diapers if you or your partner becomes incontinent.

What was your biggest takeaway from this chapter?

24

REAL LIFE SITUATIONS
WHEN S*&% HITS THE FAN

D ealing with real life situations is life, every day. Some situations are minute to minute, weekly, monthly, or yearly. Some come skidding into your life from out of nowhere, like a car accident or a job loss.

Life happens.

How you and your partner react and respond says a lot about you, your relationship, and how you deal with real life.

Recording your answers in this book is handy, right?

Review your answers and delve into the reasons why.

How do you handle sudden changes?

Go with the flow?

Get angry?

. . .

Overreact?

Melt down?

Remain calm?

Address with a positive attitude?

Are you a procrastinator?

Are you proactive or reactive?

Do you plan, or sit back and let things fall where they may?

Are you flexible or set in stone?

How do you handle resentment toward yourself or others?

How do you deal with rejection?

Do you internalize it?

Do you vent? If so, how?

. . .

How do you deal with disappointment?

Do you blame others?

Do you throw your frustration outward toward an innocent party?

Do you accept and acknowledge your mistakes and correct them?

Do you apologize when needed?

Do you hold yourself accountable when wrong?

How do you handle confrontations?

How do you handle constructive criticism or feedback?

Are you a know-it-all?

How do you handle tragedy or trauma?

Would you shut down or shut others out?

Would you self-medicate to drown out feelings or pain?

. . .

Self-medicating can include many different things like drugs, alcohol, gambling, shopping or affairs.

Would you get professional help if you feel you need it?

Below are some real-life scenarios that could occur during a relationship.
Put yourself in both positions when you read the scenario and determine how you would react and handle it.

Scenario #1:

You find out that your partner was having a physical affair for the last six months. You find out, confront them, and then they confess and want a second chance.

What do you do?

- Offer a second chance?
- Forgive?
- Get counseling together?
- Go alone?
- Can you trust him/her again?
- Leave the relationship?

Scenario #2:

Your partner is arrested for a first time for driving under the influence (DUI), but no accident or injury is involved.

What would you do?

- Would you bail your partner out?
- Let them wait?
- Freak out?
- Do you feel angry, sad, disgusted?
- Does this affect your perception of them?
- Do you resent them for financial impact and inconvenience this will cause?
- Do you decide to forgive them, really forgive?
- Do you let go and not bring up the DUI incident later?

Scenario #3:

Your partner gains a lot of weight during your relationship and you are no longer physically attracted to them.

What would you do?

- Would you try and help them lose the weight?
- What if they don't want to lose the weight or don't care?
- Would you voice your concerns regarding their eating habits when they make food choices?
- Would you tell them you are no longer attracted to them?
- Would you withhold affection?
- Would you have an affair?
- Would you threaten to leave?
- Would you end the relationship?

Scenario #4:

How would you and your partner deal with an unplanned pregnancy before marriage or before making a serious commitment?

How would you come to an understanding or agreement?

- Stay together (unmarried) and have the baby?
- Get married and raise the baby?
- Have the baby and give up for adoption?
- End the pregnancy?
- End the relationship?

What was your biggest takeaway from this chapter?

25

DISSECTION OF A RED FLAG
(ARF)

During the beginning of your relationship bliss, your beloved can do no wrong. This timeframe in a new relationship is the ARF avoidance period. You will be unable or unwilling to see the obvious. I fondly refer to these behaviors or traits as a red flag (ARF).

When ARF appears, you rationalize the behavior as quirky, easily justified, or my favorite reaction, you just dismiss it.

ARF is what you choose to ignore now and regret later.

We blindly look past ARF or two or seven while wearing "denial goggles" or "lust blinders" and try to convince ourselves of one of the following:

1. The behavior or trait will go away
2. They will change
3. They will change for me
4. I can change or fix him/her
5. Stay in complete denial (my personal favorite)

Not all people or relationships have ARF; but we are human. We have life experiences that mold us into who we are.

It is the type or nature of ARF and how it presents itself that really matters.

Someone who has a mental illness under control with medication is not ARF.

Someone who hides their mental illness and medicates it with Crystal Meth is. That's when you might want to assume another identity and run.

The genuine stories shared here are to hopefully enlighten and ultimately guide you to seeing ARF by removing denial goggles. Being able and willing to acknowledge what is in your partner or relationship enables you to make educated decisions and choices. In addition, these stories stimulate reflection on how you might react if you encounter any of these situations.

Five hot-topic red flags:

- Unfaithfulness
- Addiction
- Lawbreaking
- Jealously/Possessiveness
- Domestic Violence

These five red flags are what most people would probably not want to admit to, either due to shame or fear of rejection. There are also many who don't care, don't want to acknowledge, change, or own their red flags. If any of these are ARF that is present, they will eventually come creeping out at some point, especially if you choose to wear "denial goggles."

If you take off the "denial goggles," you will hopefully see the red flags and be able to make an educated decision.

. . .

Have you worn "denial goggles" in the past?

If yes, what was red flag trait or behavior that you chose to ignore?

Why did you choose to ignore the red flag?

What is your takeaway from recognizing your past red flag avoidance behavior?

True story ~ Common Denominator

So, I have this friend. There was no way she was at fault for the failure of her relationships...or so she thought. No, she wasn't at fault, it was her partners who were unfaithful. However, the one thing she did do was choose these men.

If you are noticing a pattern of selecting a new partner only to have your relationships fail again, you might just be the common denominator. There are many types of common denominators in failing relationships.

Pick apart the dynamics and the timeline of your past relationships:

What caused the relationship to fail?

Was it a combination of things or one big blow-out issue like infidelity?

. . .

See if anything starts to stand out as a pattern. Changing your future choices comes from growth and acknowledgement of the past. This usually leads to the ability to detect ARF right away instead of keeping the denial goggles on.

Is your pen or pencil still out? Be ready to take some notes, especially if anything pops out from these true events.

The Unfaithful Player

If you suspect your partner is being unfaithful, you are probably right. Your gut instincts are more accurate than you might think.

Do you have real proof of your partner's infidelity?

Do you need physical proof?

Do you really want to know, or would you rather keep wearing "denial goggles"?

If you are dealing with a very manipulative or narcissistic personality, proof probably won't matter as they will try to talk their way out of it anyway.

> The player. Aka a cheater. Player or cheater—both equally unfaithful, which *is defined as "engaging in sexual relations with a person other than one's regular partner in contravention of a previous promise or understanding."* [1]

Below is a list of possible signs that you might be with a cheater:

- Secretive phone use. They won't leave phone unattended, unlocked or has more than one cell phone. They may have social media accounts, email, phone apps and dating sites that you are unaware of.
- Lying starts with small fibs that grow larger and more frequent
- Missing gaps of time when they are out (trips to the store that last for hours or they tell you they got a flat tire on the way home)
- Works late, works overtime, or changes shifts when it is out of character for them or their job
- Tells you they went to Target but comes back with a bag from Walmart.
- Missing money, cash withdrawals or has unexplained charges on the credit card
- Nights out with the boys/girls, but none of their friends have been out with them
- Picks a fight with you so they can justify storming out of the house and be gone for hours or overnight
- Takes a sudden interest in their appearance like working out, or trying different clothing, a new hair style, contact lenses, etc.
- Less talkative and doesn't want to spend as much time with you
- Has a new hobby or a hobby that doesn't seem to fit them
- Goes golfing, fishing, or dog walking without bringing golf clubs, fishing poles, or the dog
- When you question them about certain sketchy behaviors, they call you crazy or insecure and make you question your sanity. This is known as gaslighting.
- Comes home and goes straight to the shower
- Can't stay with you overnight at your place
- Won't let you come over to their place...because they tell

you it's being renovated. Not! It's because their partner or spouse is at their home.
- Avoids certain restaurants or venues so not to be seen with you
- Less interest in sex because they are getting it elsewhere
- Has scratch marks or a hickey...ouch!
- Calls out another person's name during sex...double ouch!!
- Gives you a STD...triple ouch!!!

If you do find out you are being cheated on, it may shock you or just confirm what you suspected deep down. Sometimes just acknowledging the infidelity is the hardest part because it just plain hurts.

There are plenty of love gone wrong, cheating, and revenge songs born from that pain. Just remember that slashing tires and leather seats are just words from *Carrie* Underwood's *song*, "Before He Cheats". It is not a recommendation.

Please don't destroy property or hurt someone if you get hurt. Karma always works its way around.

Who wants to admit they have been cheated on? No one. It's devastating to our heart, self-esteem, and feelings of trust. Many couples do survive infidelity and thrive. Know what you are willing to live with. Be true to yourself and your heart.

True Story ~ Bidding Appointment

So, I have this friend. Jennifer fell for a bad boy. He was tall, good looking, and appeared to be successful. Note the word appeared. Bill has his own construction company. He rode a fast motorcycle and pushed the limits. Jennifer fell so hard, it knocked her brains down to her perfectly manicured toes. Sound familiar?

She didn't see ARF. Her choice was to stay in complete denial.

Bill tells her that his customers owe him money, but he hasn't been paid yet. So, she financially helps him out, after he moves into her place. Time goes on and they are engaged. So, it's fine that she gave him a large sum of money, because now they're getting married. They muddle along until he starts acting shadier than usual.

Eventually, Jennifer decides to download an app on his phone which sent her his texts, phone calls, and browsing history.

Let's just say it didn't even take a day for her to discover the shady business he was conducting.

He was actually selling himself to "cougars," older women with lots of discretionary income. That was how he was making money. All the bidding appointments he went to, that interestingly never ended up in construction contracts, were actually sex-for-hire appointments.

Jennifer ended the relationship. It was soul-crushing and trust-shattering. Here's the thing, technology has made it so easy to be shady. You can have multiple email accounts, text to email, burner cell phones, and apps that cover shady business and secret dating sites.

Someone who is attached to their device and won't put them down while going to the bathroom might have something to hide. It begins and ends with trust. You should be open to letting your partner see everything if they ask.

Everything, all of it: phone, email, social media, laptop, etc. If not, you probably have something to hide.

Transparency—ugh—I am so sick of this word. It is beyond overused, but it's actually the best fit here. Transparency is exactly what you need to give and have if you want complete intimacy.

True Story ~ Unlock Code

So, I have this friend. Linda's man was completely attached to his phone. He wouldn't leave the room without it. Linda had her own phone, but one day the battery was dead. She asked to borrow her man's phone to make a quick call, and he literally came unglued. He berated her for not keeping her phone charged properly. When he finally relented, he made sure he was right there when she used the phone. There was no time for her to see any texts or pictures.

His behavior was a red flag and fortunately for Linda, she acknowledged it. When he fell asleep, she checked his phone after memorizing the unlock code (smart girl). It was full of text and pics from other girls. He was a player. As much as it hurt her, she dumped him.

Pay attention to the time your partner spends on their device and see if they have an open device policy. It shouldn't be hard to figure out if they are hiding something.

Addiction

Addiction is one of the most stressful relationship red flags. Being with someone who is in recovery is a lifetime commitment. Addicts are never "cured" and they deal with maintaining sobriety forever. The addict can inflict the worst mental and physical stress on their partner. In addition, they may be on a self-destruction mission and won't care who they take down with them.

True Story ~ Disappear

I have a friend whose husband went on three-to-four-day drug binges that mentally, physically, and emotionally screwed with her while she tried to raise two kids and work. He would just disappear for days.

Jon just didn't come home from work one day and remained missing for three gut-wrenching days. This is a guy who went to work every day for the nine years they had been married. His ARF was being a recovering drug addict. Her ARF reaction was that the behavior or trait would go away.

To Morgan, her husband's addiction was in the past and would never resurface, so Morgan initially thought he'd been in an accident. After frantically searching for 24 hours, his coworker tells her that he is probably just "getting high." What the hell? Morgan lies to the kids and tells them their dad is working out of town.

Morgan doesn't sleep or eat for three days. Funny how the addict uses drugs to stay up and the spouse stays up on pure stress, caffeine, and adrenaline. Jon finally arrived home and is "coming down." She has never seen him display such irrational behavior.

Jon says it was a one-time relapse and Morgan wanted to believe him.

The drug-binging pattern repeated itself two more times over the next twelve months. Morgan loses twenty pounds that she didn't need to lose in the first place and lives on the brink of sanity from sleep deprivation. Deep down Morgan knew it might not end. The next time he disappeared, she left.

Many recovering addicts stay in recovery. Unfortunately, for Morgan her husband's red flag came back with a vengeance.

True Story ~ He'll Change

So, I have this friend. Beth married her high school sweetheart, Mark. They partied together when they met, but Beth grew up and out of it. Mark never did. Beth loved being a wife and mother. They had three kids, and by the time the youngest was two, Mark was a semi-functioning alcoholic.

Beth's ARF was that he would change after having kids.

AA.org - Alcoholics Anonymous

Al-Anon.org or (888) 425-2666 – Help and resources for the friends and families of problem drinkers/alcoholics/addicts

NA.org - Narcotics Anonymous

1-800-GAMBLER - Free, confidential help

cdph.ca.gov/

Lawbreaker

If your partner has committed illegal acts in the past and they have learned and reformed, this red flag is "in the past" and hopefully will not resurface. However, if you feel your partner is engaging in illegal activity, run a background check and check public records. This is a bonus of living in the age of technology.

It is usually during our teen or young adult years when law boundaries may get pushed because we feel invincible.

The majority of people grow up and become law-abiding. But a percentage of people will continue to make poor choices, commit crimes, end up in jail, prison, or on parole and unable to function in mainstream society.

If you decide to have a relationship with someone who engages in unlawful behaviors, they will most likely take you down as well. Basically, avoid this red flag at all costs; otherwise, it could cost you.

This leads us to the "bad boy" syndrome. The guy who is always in some sort of trouble, but he says he's innocent and misunderstood. The bad boy is the guy who gets to you because you probably have low self-esteem. He is the salesman type who can make you believe the bra you found in his car *is* actually yours.

Real men are good, stand-up men with productive lives. Bad boys are just that, "boys" who never grow up. They use women and make excuses for their poor lot in life. Women can be just as "bad" and use men.

There are no gender preferences for poor, senseless behavior.

Jealously and Possessiveness

Oh, isn't it cute that my partner is jealous?

It just means they really love me.

No, it doesn't.

This person has emotional issues that usually stem from deep-seated insecurities or possible psychosis. Be very aware and be ready to run if they check your cell phone, follow you or your family and friends, or show up at your work or your home unannounced.

This is called stalking.

Stalking is a form of intimidation and also a crime.

If they alienate you from your friends and family, don't just walk...run away! This is not normal, even if your family is awful.

If your partner dictates what you wear, who you hang out with and when, this is not healthy. Demanding you change your outfit, your hair, or your plans is ARF.

Controlling and stalking issues aren't just saved for men. Women are sometimes "cray, cray" jealous, too.

Everyone feels jealously at one time or another. It's natural.

We all want the new girlfriend to have bad skin, a big nose, and cellulite. What is not natural are controlling behaviors or irrational actions that can ensue because of possessiveness and jealousy.

True Story ~ Amiss

So, I have this friend. Dylan started dating a new girl, Lillian. They went out for a few weeks and then Dylan just sort of dropped off the face of the earth. His friends can't get him to hang out anymore and he's missed the last two family functions. At first, everyone just thinks it's because the relationship is new.

But as time goes by, nothing changes, and his mother and brother get concerned. Dylan lies and says they are just busy. The truth is that Lillian is manipulating him away from his family and friends so he will spend every minute just with her.

At first, he loves all her attention and affection, but as time passes, Dylan wants to venture out of the "Lillian" circle and Lillian then revolts. She cries or yells or does whatever it takes to get him to spend all his time with her. At this point, it is just easier to give in than to keep fighting with her. Bottom line: she wins.

Dylan's ARF was that the behavior or trait would go away.

Finally, Dylan's brother showed up at Dylan's workplace and pointed out the possessiveness Lillian was inflicting on him. Dylan finally broke up with her and it got even uglier.

She stalked him, harassed his mother, accused her of instigating the breakup, and lastly, showed up at Dylan's workplace. Lillian told anyone that would listen she was pregnant (she wasn't) and how Dylan had dumped her when she told him.

Suggestion: Being controlled, stalked, or treated like a possession is the farthest thing from love. Please acknowledge this to yourself if you experience anything that sounds like what is written above.

Ask your family and friends and people that know you, if they love you, they will tell you if they think something is amiss. When I say amiss, I mean a freaking mess. Get out. These behaviors can easily lead to domestic violence.

True Story ~ Demand Much

My friend Leslie's husband could not handle any criticism and was very possessive. She later found out it was due to deep-seated insecurity, even though he always appeared to be extremely put-together. He always presented a strong façade.

In addition, his expectations for Leslie were unrealistic.

An example of this was that Leslie was berated on a regular basis if she didn't answer her cell phone immediately or reply to text messages quickly. He would immediately accuse her of cheating if she didn't reply to every text or call instantly. Leslie was frequently checking her phone, which created an extreme level of anxiety and left Leslie a nervous wreck.

Domestic Violence

A close personal friend of jealousy and possessiveness is domestic violence. There are many types of domestic violence.

Here are some examples:

- Mentally abuses you- threatens to hurt or kill you, your kids, your family and friends. Stalks you, your family, and friends
- Intimidates via threats- causing you to do things you

would not do like committing crimes or lying to police to protect yourself, your kids, and family.
- Physically assaults you- grabbing, choking, pushing, punching, shaking, pulling, dragging, hitting, scratching, biting, slapping, burning, raping, stabbing, shooting, etc.

The domestic violence ARF didn't show up in my friend Nikki's relationship right away, but its cousins jealously and possessiveness were there from the start and she chose to think that he'd change for her on the red flag avoidance scale. She thought if she loved him enough, he'd feel secure and not be jealous.

She was wrong.

No one can change anyone else.

The other person must want to change for themselves; you can only change yourself.

Domestic violence is a type of abuse. It can be the abuse of a spouse or partner, which is also known as intimate partner violence. Or it could be the abuse of a child, older relative, or other family member.

Domestic violence may include different types of abuse, such as:

- **Physical violence** that can lead to injuries such as bruises or fractures (broken bones)
- **Sexual violence**, including sexual assault
- **Emotional abuse**, which includes threats, name-calling, put-downs, and humiliation. It can also involve controlling behavior, such as telling the victim how to act or dress and not letting them see family or friends.
- **Economic abuse**, which involves controlling access to money
- **Stalking**, which is repeated, unwanted contact that causes fear or concern for the safety of the victim. This can include watching or following the victim. The stalker may send repeated, unwanted phone calls or texts.[2]

Know this, fear does not belong in a relationship.

Recognize and acknowledge ARF that makes you feel unsafe.

Maintaining your own safety and self-worth is paramount. Many victims of domestic violence have usually had unfortunate life experiences that have left them feeling unworthy.

Consider talking to someone you trust or calling the hotlines listed. If Nikki had acknowledged the jealous/possessive ARF from the beginning, I'd like to think she would have never experienced domestic violence.

The National Domestic Violence Hotline
   Call 24/7
   1-800-799-7233 (SAFE)
   1-800-787-3224 (TTY for Deaf/hard of hearing)

Extraction

If you have decided to end an unhealthy or abusive relationship and need to extract yourself, please carefully read further.

It will depend on the nature of ARF you have encountered, to determine how easy or difficult the extraction process might be. Be sure to get help, reach out to family, friends, law enforcement, social services, therapists, and hotlines if needed. Do not go it alone, especially if you have even the slightest feelings of fear.

If you have been or are dealing with a volatile situation, don't go it alone. Seek help and take help with you.

Please consider the following:

- Tell your family and friends you are ending the relationship.
- Break off the relationship in a public place quickly – do not drag out the process.
- Have a friend or family member nearby to step in and get you out if necessary.
- If you live with the person, be prepared to leave your

house if the other person won't leave. It's also good to have someone with you.
- Bring someone with you if need to pack up.
- Make a clean break.
- Block calls, text, social media, emails etc. (change you phone number and email if necessary)
- Get counseling or therapy for yourself and your kids, if necessary.
- Get professional help such as legal assistance or a restraining order if necessary, or a shelter for abused women/children.

What is your biggest takeaway from this chapter?

26

DEAL BREAKERS

Deal breakers, like "must haves," should not be superficial in nature. It should not matter if the love of your life has green eyes or brown. Deal breakers are boundaries.

We need them to protect who we are.

Without them we can become pretzels, co-dependent, and develop low self-esteem.

Think about the rest of your life. If you are looking for the one and done dream, you must know and stand by your deal breakers.

Maybe your deal breaker is you don't want kids. This is a huge decision that should be honored.

If your partner feels like they can change your mind later, where does that leave you?

Did you waste your time?

This is why you should define what is truly a deal breaker for you in a relationship.

List your top 3 deal breakers:
1.
2.
3.

So, I have this friend. Katie's deal breakers are solid and she will not waver as she evaluates potential partners.

Katie's deal breakers are:

1. Non-smoker
2. Needs the same religion
3. Does not want children

What was your biggest takeaway from this chapter?

27

WRAP IT UP

The life stories shared here are to enlighten you, making you aware of the ideas, questions, scenarios, and red flags you may have never thought of before.

If you are open to learning, you will acquire knowledge. With knowledge comes the ability to make educated choices.

Knowledge is power.

With all these stories, important life lessons were learned. These stories with lessons showed individuals who developed courage, strength, and the ability to try again.

What is this life without giving, receiving, and inspiring love?

List at least 5 of your exceptional traits:

Do you think you have areas that might need some personal improvement? If yes, list them here:

When you feel love, you feel hope.

My hope is when you begin to feel love you slow down a little and take the necessary time to be sure about to whom you are giving your precious heart.

Asking the rough-around-the-edges questions isn't necessarily to edit out the person or end the relationship. Asking questions helps you find out if you are able and willing to continue when you have a deeper knowledge of the person you are falling for.

It has been my deep honor to share these stories with you.

With gratitude,
Leah Kay Rossi

REFERENCES

8. Finances

1. Stewart Welch. "The #1 Reason for Divorce?" *Advance Local*. Updated March 7, 2019. https://www.al.com/business/2018/07/the_1_reason_for_divorce.html#:~:text=And%20while%20the%20reasons%20vary,debilitate%20individuals%20and%20devastate%20families.

10. Mental Health

1. Source: U.S. National Library of Medicine.

20. Marriage, In-laws, & Family

1. "Marriage and Divorce," American Psychological Association, accessed May 8, 2021, https://www.apa.org/topics/divorce-child-custody#:~:text=However%2C%20about%2040%20to%2050,subsequent%20marriages%20is%20even%20higher.

25. Dissection of A Red Flag

1. "Unfaithful," Google Dictionary, Accessed May 8, 2021, https://www.google.com/search?q=unfaithful+definition&oq=unfaithful+def&aqs=chrome.0.0j69i57j0l3j0i22i30l5.2886j0j15&sourceid=chrome&ie=UTF-8
2. Source: U.S. National Library of Medicine.

ACKNOWLEDGMENTS

I want to thank the hundreds of real stories and events that were shared with me as I began my research. They came from the trust imparted by those who opened up and bared their hurts, hopes and dreams to me. Without their willingness to confide, this book would not exist to serve its purpose of helping others.

I'm deeply grateful to all those who have loved, lost and still never gave up.

Thank you to the original Bailey girls whose input and support were invaluable as they bore witness to the endless hours of writing on yellow notepads and countless edits. They watched and encouraged me as I embarked on this journey.

I hope the information in this book inspires someone's decision or path.

Thank you to the family and friends that never gave up on me when my love life could have been scripted from a bad reality television show.

And thank you to you, the reader, for being willing to open yourself up to what is next.

With gratitude and love,

L. K. Rossi

ABOUT THE AUTHOR

Leah Kay Rossi's passion for writing comes from the hope that others can have the tools she spent so much of her life without. Her strongest desire is that one of the ideas, thoughts, or suggestions contained in her writing will impact and empower readers in a positive way.

Readers can continue to connect with Leah by visiting her blog at https://leahkayrossi.blog.

www.ingramcontent.com/pod-product-compliance
Lightning Source LLC
Chambersburg PA
CBHW072013110526
44592CB00012B/1295